IN QUEST OF HASTED

IN QUEST OF
HASTED

John Boyle

Phillimore

1984

Published by
PHILLIMORE AND CO. LTD.
Shopwyke Hall, Chichester, Sussex

ISBN 0 85033 557 4

Printed and bound in Great Britain by
THE CAMELOT PRESS LTD.
Southampton, England

CONTENTS

LIST OF PLATES

(between pages 52 and 53)

LIST OF TEXT ILLUSTRATIONS

ACKNOWLEDGEMENTS

My involvement with the papers of Edward Hasted came about quite by accident when Anne Oakley, the Cathedral and City Archivist of Canterbury deputed me to examine and report on certain documents deposited in the Cathedral library; they proved to be the working papers and correspondence of the historian of Kent. Miss Oakley gave me full facilities (including her own expert advice) to carry out a full and detailed study of the material when, but for her many other commitments, she would obviously have liked to undertake the task herself. When my searches took me to repositories outside Canterbury I received help from other people, some of whose names are mentioned in my text. In certain last-minute (but very important) researches Miss M. M. Condon and Mr. D. Crook of the Public Record Office gave vital assistance.

Encouragement is as important as practical help, and this I received from many quarters, some, in view of the trend of my enquiries, quite unexpected. Particularly welcome was the approval of those two stalwarts of Kentish historiography, Frank and Ronald Jessup.

To all have thus guided, assisted, and heartened me on my way I express my heartfelt gratitude.

PICTORIAL ACKNOWLEDGEMENTS

Mrs. T. C. Mallik kindly loaned the delightful study of St John's (No. 1). Other photographs are reproduced by courtesy of the British Library (Nos. 2 and 11–21); the *Kentish Gazette* (No. 3); Rochester upon Medway City Council (No. 4); the author is responsible for Nos. 5–10. The text illustrations are reproduced by permission of the Dean and Chapter of Canterbury (Nos. 1–4, 7 and 9), and of the Kent County Archivist (Nos. 10, 12 and 14).

EDWARD HASTED

Born 31 December 1732, in London
Died 14 January 1812, at Corsham, Wilts.

The History and Topographical Survey of the County of Kent

First (Folio) Edition

Volume I	1778
Volume II	1782
Volume III	1790
Volume IV	1799

Second (Octavo) Edition

Volumes 1–3	1797
Volumes 4–7	1798
Volume 8	1799
Volumes 9–11	1800
Volume 12	1801

Chapter One

THE MAKING OF A LEGEND

FOR ANYONE visiting it for the first time Corsham in Wiltshire is a place of pleasant surprises. To a complete stranger 'Corsham, Wilts.' might conjure up an image of a little hamlet nestling amid the downs, but he will find a small town, complete with town hall, set in the lush, well-wooded country nearing the Somerset border. It is indeed a charming place, whose main advantages have been a plentiful supply of Bath stone, a tradition of dignified architecture and a freedom from discordant modern development. 'Corsham', says an authority, 'has no match in Wiltshire for wealth of good houses.'

A Kentish pilgrim to the place where his county's historian, Edward Hasted, ended his days might half expect to find his enquiries met with a blank stare and professions of ignorance; in fact, on the experience of at least one such pilgrim, he will find Hasted's memory still green, with an account of documents about him being lately recognised and borne off to County Hall at Trowbridge to be kept safely in the archives.

Perhaps the greatest surprise of all is to find associations of that extraordinary character, Customer Smith, so often mentioned in Hasted's pages; he it was who built Corsham Court in the days of Elizabeth I. Thomas Smith (or Smythe) was a haberdasher and collector of the customs of London who, from the fortune he made, was nicknamed 'the Customer'. He migrated to Kent where he built other impressive residences, and made what are described as 'magnificent additions' to Westenhanger, the ancient fortified house whose ruins can be seen next to the Folkestone racecourse.

Near the gates of the stately avenue leading down from Corsham Court are the dignified stone-built Hungerford almshouses, in which Edward Hasted ended his life as Master. It was here in the year 1812, when the Peninsular War was at its height and Napoleon was preparing that fatal campaign against Russia, that Hasted departed this life, having by a codicil to his will bequeathed the manuscripts concerning his *History* to his friend of long standing, Dr. William Boteler of Eastry in East Kent.

The making of a will is a not unusual precaution amongst people who have anything to leave; less common is that of writing one's own obituary, but Hasted had taken this one also, and left a suitable account of himself with instructions as to its use, thus launching the Hasted legend on its way:

> I request my Executor to cause the following insertion immediately after my death, to be sent for that purpose to the Publisher of the *Gentleman's Magazine*, to

be inserted in the Obituary of the next Magazine after my death; and I am sure my much-respected friend Mr. Nichols will have the goodness to consent to it:

'Edward Hasted, Esq., was the only son of Edward Hasted, of Hawley, Kent, Esq., barrister-at-law; descended paternally from the noble family of Clifford, as he was maternally from the ancient and knightly family of the Dingleys of Woolverton, in the Isle of Wight. His laborious *History of Kent* took him up more than 40 years, during the whole series of which he spared neither pains nor expence to bring it to maturity; and the reputation which it still maintains in the judgment of the public is the best proof of its merits. Notwithstanding his attention to this his favourite object during the whole of the above time, he acted as a magistrate and a deputy lieutenant for the county of Kent with uncommon zeal and activity. He was F.R.S. and S.A. In the latter part of his life he felt the pressure of adverse fortune, which obliged him to quit his residence in Kent, after which he lived in obscure retirement, and for some time in the environs of London, noticed by a few valuable friends, from whom he received constant tokens of benevolent friendship, as having known him in more fortunate circumstances, several of whom are of the rank of nobility, and of high estimation in life. A few years ago, his honourable and highly respected patron and friend, the Earl of Radnor, presented him to the Mastership of the Hospital at Corsham in Wiltshire (a most desirable asylum), to which he then removed; and having obtained, a few years ago, the chancellor's decree for the recovery of his estates in Kent, of which he had been defrauded, it enabled him again to enjoy the sweets of an independent competence during the remainder of his life. He died at the Master's Lodge at the Lady Hungerford's Hospital, in Corsham, Wilts., at the advanced age of 80, Jan. 14, 1812. By Anne, his wife, who died in 1803, Mr. Hasted left four sons and two daughters, of whom the eldest son is now a respectable clergyman, vicar of Hollingbourne (with the chapel of Hucking annexed) near Maidstone, in Kent . . .'.

'In lapidary inscriptions a man is not upon oath', said Dr. Johnson, and Hasted, an admirer of Johnson, may have had this comment in mind when writing what was to serve as his own epitaph (for he had no other). It was perhaps therefore excusable to describe a seven-year sojourn in the King's Bench debtors' prison as 'living in obscure retirement'.

Having made these and other appropriate dispositions, Hasted, as we have said, departed this mortal scene. His son, writing to the Earl of Radnor, spoke of the suddenness of his father's decease, so that we may hope that he was spared any prolonged suffering. His obituary was published as he had wished, and his papers departed from the public view and indeed from public knowledge.

Although Hasted does not say so in the obituary, there were actually two editions of the *History* during his lifetime. Indeed, the demand for a second edition made itself heard before he had finished writing the first one, a fact on which Hasted's admirers rightly set great store.

The first edition was published by subscription, and the list of subscribers occupies four pages. It includes many members of the peerage, and also a number of people whose names will crop up in this account: William Boys, Thomas Astle, Sir Brook Bridges, William Deedes, Dr. Ducarel, Bryan Faussett, Richard Gough, the Earl of Radnor, Sir Sidney S. Smythe (a descendant of 'the Customer'), Simmons and Kirby (printers); others were Richard Harris Barham, the humorous poet, Dr. Beauvoir (celebrated headmaster of the King's School, Canterbury), C. R. Bunce, the archivist, The Lord Archbishop of Canterbury, the Dean and

Chapter of Canterbury, Francis Grose (writer and illustrator, friend of Robert Burns and described as the 'antiquarian Falstaff'), Francis Austen, great-uncle of the famous Jane, several college libraries both of Oxford and Cambridge, a resident of Jamaica, John Morse, and the Headmaster of Westminster School.

The first edition was of four volumes in the massive folio size, 3,335 pages in all. Of this huge mass of writing about a hundred and fifty pages were devoted to 'The General History of Kent', the balance being entitled 'A topographical Survey, or History, of the several Laths and Hundreds in the County of Kent and of each particular Town and Parish within the same'.

The 'General History of Kent' is treated by Hasted as introductory matter, paged in Roman numerals, its narrative interrupted by accounts of the holders of various offices and dignities, with brief biographies of the more important figures such as the Kings and Earls of Kent, short particulars of the sheriffs, and a list of the Knights of the Shire and the Justices of the Peace in the various reigns. There are essays on such matters of organisation of the realm under the Saxon kings, the offices of coroner, sheriff and Justice of the Peace, the administrative divisions and geography of the county and its ecclesiastical organisation. A disquisition on feudal land tenures including, naturally, Kent's special custom of gavelkind, is followed by a section on the religious houses and their dissolution at the Reformation, and finally by an account of the Kent entries in Domesday Book.

The general scheme of the 'Topographical Survey' is as follows: the descriptions of the 'laths' and hundreds are quite perfunctory, amounting to little more than a list of hundreds within each lath, and of the parishes and places within each hundred. The descriptions of the towns and cities follow no fixed pattern, depending as they do on the special features of each place; but the accounts of the parishes conform very much to a set plan, based fundamentally on the descents of the ownerships of the manors and other important properties. Topographical details are meagre, and social history almost non-existent. If the place is mentioned in the Domesday Book an extract is printed; the ecclesiastical organisation and history of the parish are treated very fully.

One does not know how many millions of words there were because the number of pages does not tell the whole story; the book was noteworthy for the enormous number and length of the footnotes which were in a small type and therefore increased the number of words incalculably. There were even footnotes to footnotes. The second edition consisted of no less than 12 substantial volumes in the smaller octavo format.

After Hasted's death his reputation as an historian fluctuated as the years rolled by. The first attack on it came soon after the appearance of his obituary in the *Gentleman's Magazine*. Writing in August 1812, 'Litterator' softened his criticism with a certain padding of faint praise. 'Hasted's great Topographical work has much merit. As an history of the property of the county, it is in my opinion a wonderful performance; as containing its genealogies it is entitled to much, but no unqualified praise. But when we have said this, have we not exhausted all its claims to commendation? Mr. Hasted was well acquainted with records; and in the earlier part of his life very diligent in extracting materials from them; which, in the hurry of his last composition, he has made but an imperfect use of. But he wanted all the higher qualities of an Historian: the manners and the arts he had little perception of; he neither possessed the talents of biography, nor felt much curiosity regarding it; his local inquiries have opened no neglected literary notices; and he, who turns to all this mass of personal memorials, must still resort to other means for separating the eminent from the obscure.' Litterator complains that the literary achievements of the Kentish gentry in the 17th century 'will not be found, or very imperfectly found, in Hasted's voluminous pages', and concludes with the jibe that he (Litterator) has 'not much taste for the history of a county's mere landholders or its mere squires'.

In the September issue Litterator returned to the attack: 'The fault of Hasted is that he has no variety: all is reduced to one dull narrative, consisting of little more than a dull deduction of the Proprietors of Manors in a kind of language which forms nothing like a style, but savours most of the technicalities of an attorney's office . . . With him, one man only differs from another by his name, the date of his birth, and death; and the family into which he married; unless we add his rent-roll, and the specification of the manors of which he was the owner'.

A slashing counter-attack was not long in coming: in the November issue, writing from the *Leather Bottle Inn,* Northfleet, the Chairman of the Kent Natural History Society (who otherwise remains anonymous) expresses strong resentment at Litterator's 'ill-timed reflection on the best of Kentish Historians'. If Hasted's history is deficient, why does not Litterator write an additional volume himself? Shades of Johnson—'You may scold a carpenter who has made you a bad table, though you cannot make a table'. Hasted, says our Chairman, deserves the thanks of posterity for communicating to it new information that it took nearly half a century to collect. 'Who else could have done this?' As to dullness, what can you expect from a county history? A fairy tale? Tristram Shandy? The descent of the manors the Chairman had recently found useful to answer a problem that was worrying him concerning Cobham College. He quotes extensively (from the octavo edition evidently) to rebut Litterator's assertion that Hasted was uninterested in nature, art, or people's characters, and recalls giving at a scientific society's dinner a toast 'To the memory of Mr. Hasted, for his *History of Kent'.*

The last shot in this literary skirmish is fired by 'An Old Correspondent' who is enthusiastically devoted to the Hasted cause; compared with other county histories, no one would select Hasted's as being pre-eminent for dullness (writes Old Correspondent). Manorial descents and genealogies are traditional features of such books, and require knowledge of legal technicalities. And a good thing too, he seems to think, pleasing alike to members of old families and to men trying to found new ones, whose feelings 'will not be shaken by the sneers of modern Philosophy'.

From 1834 onward a more critical tone was set by the patronising and unflattering opinions written into the autobiography of Sir Samuel Egerton Brydges, an able man and fastidious publisher at his private printing press at Lee Priory near Canterbury, but somewhat of a rogue withal and noteworthy for his spiteful pen; he describes his fellow-residents in East Kent as mean, bigoted, ignorant and clannish, and some of them 'sprung from the very dregs of the people'. In his sketch of Edward Hasted, to whom he concedes the title of 'The Historian of Kent', the perjorative epithets flow freely from Brydges' pen; he describes Hasted as 'a voluble and flighty talker' who did not secure respect for his knowledge: 'hasty', 'careless', 'reckless', 'unsteady', and 'imprudent in his life'. Often cited is Brydges' cryptic observation that the latter part of the *History* was brought out in a slovenly manner. He is also quoted for his unkind remarks about Hasted's appearance: 'a little mean-looking man with a long face and a high nose'. Furthermore Brydges denies the historian any imagination or sentiment, or any special quality of mind except memory.

However, even Brydges is constrained to allow some merits to the *History*. He concedes that Hasted consulted many original documents 'but not with much critical industry so that neither his descent of property, nor his genealogies will always be found minutely exact; *but altogether it is a great work*: and it is wonderful that it is done so well. I have seen no reason to suspect his honesty in its compilation'. Brydges was of the generation after that of Hasted and was at school with the historian's sons.

Brydges' integrity is suspect because of his claim, supported it seems by a certain amount of forged evidence, that his elder unmarried brother, Timewell, was entitled to the barony of Chandos. Although the claim was thrown out by the House of Lords, Brydges insisted on describing himself after his brother's death as *'per legem terrae* Baron Chandos of Sudely'.

The Victorians could not at first make up their minds about Hasted; there was some sarcastic criticism before opinion evolved into the present more favourable assessment. In 1862-3, an anonymous writer in *Archaeologia Cantiana* says that 'Hasted is generally wrong'.

In the meantime, although the greater part of the historian's papers had disappeared from public view and knowledge, a considerable quantity of Hastediana found its way into various museums and repositories, or was preserved in private hands—not only documents but also personal possessions such as his spectacles kept like sacred relics. As time went on, the flow of criticism tended to dry up and Hasted began to emerge more and more as the standard authority on Kent history up to his own period. In the years 1904 and 1905 interest seems to have welled up concerning some notebooks and letters in the Maidstone Museum. No one knew exactly how they had got into the hands of the bookseller from whom they were purchased by a well-wisher, but the Kent Archaeological Society (in successive volumes of their *Journal*) treated the readers to lengthy transcripts. First to emerge in print were the *Anecdotes of the Hasted Family* written by the historian himself in 1800. (Anecdotes in the 18th and early 19th centuries means 'unpublished material' and not spicy stories.) The printed version is preceded by some anonymous comments which challenge Hasted's claims of aristocratic descent, set out in the self-composed obituary notice, and suggests that in fact he was descended from respectable yeoman stock settled in or near Canterbury. More factually, the unknown writer summarises the story that the *Anecdotes* record, beginning with the foundation of the family fortune by Edward Hasted's grandfather, Joseph, who lived at Chatham, and recounting the early death of his father, and Edward's education at Eton and as a student of Lincoln's Inn, though never called to the Bar. Hasted married young, we hear, and after living at Canterbury for a couple of years spent a large sum of money on reconstructing the ancient house known as

St John's, a former Commandery of the Military Knights at Sutton-at-Hone, near Dartford. This outlay was doubly injudicious since Hasted held a lease only of the house.[1] About 1776 he handed St John's back to the owners since he was now living at Canterbury. Then we come to what is referred to as Hasted's 'misconduct'. In 1785 he began an affair with a young girl named Mary Jane Town; the commentator skips lightly over the upshot: the historian's desertion of his wife Anne, his flight to France, enforced return, arrest and commitment to prison for debt in 1795, where he remained until he obtained his discharge (to use his own words) in 1802. A few years later he was appointed to the mastership at Corsham.

The *Anecdotes* were published somewhat apologetically owing to the unpleasing light they were considered to throw on Hasted's character and on his treatment of his mother and his wife. The commentator notes the lack of information about the writing of the *History* and condemned the vanity of the anecdotist, having in mind, perhaps, this sort of revelation: 'My father's little establishment consisted of a coachman and footman, livery servants, three maid servants and a housekeeper . . . to these I may add an upper and an under gardener. He had a coach and chariot, three coach horses, a riding horse for himself and one for his servant and three cows . . . the livery he gave his servants were a light blue suit with small gilt buttons'.

Another example that may have irritated the commentator is Hasted's account of the social distinctions prevailing in the precincts of Canterbury Cathedral in his day: 'The rank and credit I then lived in as a man of fortune and a magistrate gained her (his mother) the acquaintance of the best families of the clergy and gentry within the Precincts, who would otherwise, as they are but apt at all times, have most likely treated her as a stranger unknown to them with coldness and neglect'.

Hasted describes Anne Dorman whom he married soon after attaining his majority as a 'wife without fortune' and admits that he lived above his income and did not honour his obligation towards his mother, who had accepted an annuity in lieu of her claim to dower. Eventually, Mrs. Hasted senior took a house in London at Princes Court, near Storeys Gate in Westminster, which 'had a most pleasing view of St James's Park up to the Horse Guards at the back of it and at one end looked up the Bird Cage Walk'. When Hasted realised that he must pull his horns in and went to live in much humbler accommodation in Canterbury his mother acquiesced in his persuasions 'for her to come and reside at Canterbury'. Accordingly 'she entered into a treaty with Mr. Alderman Wilkes to assign over her lease of her house in Princes Court to him and I finished it with him for her'. If the commentator noticed that this was a reference to the great John Wilkes, writer of the *North Briton,* hero of the legal battles for press and personal freedom, duellist and devil-worshipper, who afterwards turned respectable and became Alderman and Lord Mayor of London, he kept it to himself.

The second part of Hasted's *Anecdotes,* though ambitiously headed 'Book the Second', consists of two or three pages only and it seems clear that having arrived at the year 1770 the anecdotist of the Hasted family failed to match the persistence and tenacity of the historian of Kent and proceeded to lose interest in his subject. One well-known passage, however, does occur in this brief second part of the *Anecdotes*:

I had now, about the year 1763, become acquainted upon the Habits of Intimacy with several Learned Friends, distinguished characters in the Antiquarian Line, and having thro' their means an opportunity of resorting to the Public offices of Record and other Places for obtaining collections for my *History of Kent*, which I now openly professed my Intention of Carrying forward, I, for this purpose, went with my wife to my mother's and staid there in that summer near 2 months.

We know the names of three of these 'distinguished characters': Thomas Astle, Keeper of the Records in the Tower of London and trustee of the British Museum, Dr. A. C. Ducarel, librarian of Lambeth Palace, and Sir Joseph Ayloffe, Vice-President of the Society of Antiquaries.

Hasted did manage to compose a list with dates of the most important events in his life up to 1807, the latter part of which reads as follows:

1785   Unfortunately became acquainted with Mary Jane Town.
1786   Took her into keeping and hired a House for her, 1st at Sheldwich and then at Boughton Under Blean, and then in lodgs in London, and then at Dover.
1791   Went with her to France; Boarded at St. Omers, then at Abbeville, and lastly at Calais.
1793   The War breaking out, Came to England with her, and made a Tour thro' England and stopt and boarded at Cirencester, and then returned to London and hired a House at Camden Town.
1795   Was arrested and put into the King's Bench, where she went with me.
1797   I parted with her for Infamy and Wretchedness. Harriet Brewster then came and lived with me as my servant.
1798   I was reconciled to Mrs. H. and my Family, and they came to see me.
1802   Received my Discharge, and went and Lodged in the Rules in Clarence Place and next in Greenhouse Row, where I obtained my entire freedon.
1803   Went and Lodged at Mrs. Marks opposite the Magdalen.
1804   Removed to Belvidere Pl., and thence to Greenhouse Row.
1807   Went to Corsham, being appd. Master of the Hospital there.

The startling events so coolly recorded received an equally phlegmatic commentary in *Archaeologia Cantiana*—little more than an observation that his downfall was probably due to his liaison with Mary Jane Town and not to the expenses connected with his *History*. It can be assumed therefore that the melancholy story was generally known, and the lapse in moral credit discounted in advance, so that the commentator could say, without fear of being misunderstood, that workers in the field of Kent history owed more than they often cared to own to Edward Hasted, and that his name would always be held in honour by Kentish antiquaries.

In the year of grace 1904 Kent had done Hasted proud in devoting 27 pages of *Archaeologia Cantiana* to his anecdotes. The next year it was to do even better in terms of space devoted when 'Letters of Edward Hasted to Thomas Astle' were printed. The letters were written between the years 1763 and 1800 and concern the *History* and other matters besides. One letter, at least, can scarcely have enhanced

Hasted's reputation for modesty. In December 1778, soon after a copy of his first folio volume, dedicated to King George III, had been sent to the king's librarian, Hasted wrote to Astle as follows:

> I thank you for your information relating to my Expectations from the King, pecuniary ones I never dreamt of—I only wished to know if there might not be usually some notice taken on this Occasion more than has been—as I fare the same as others I am quite Content. You are quite mistaken as to Mrs. Hasted's not being surprised at my receiving the Honor of being Dubbed, nor should I receive it at any rate till I had Consulted my good friend, Apothecary, Mayor of Maidstone, now the Worshipfull Sir Thos. Bishop, Knight, which I shall take the first opportunity of Doing, as I expect Every postboy that I see to find him a Messenger to fetch me up for this glorious purpose. I hope you have not Deceived me by flattering Tales—if you have, *Heu Quanta de spe decidi.*[2]

The highwater mark in the ebb and flow of the Hasted cult came, surely, in 1972 when, after 170 years, it was decided to publish a photographic reproduction of the second edition of the *History,* with a modern introduction. The known facts were there recounted, in the spirit, be it said, of our old friend from the *Leather Bottle,* rather than of his opponent 'Litterator', and the opportunity was taken to embroider the legend of Hasted with praiseful references to his vast and original researches, and his equally original maps based on a new survey. Further embellishments included the story of the historian's loss of his estates and financial downfall at the hands of an unscrupulous solicitor, and the subsequent recovery of the lands (somewhat diminished, apparently) on the initiative of his heroic son.

Hasted's reputation was now that of an immortal. Good critics—and not necessarily those directly connected with his county—seemed to regard his book as one of the finest county histories ever written, and after the scepticism and irony evinced in some quarters in the Victorian period he was regarded by the modern generation with reverence. He how had his place in the Kentish pantheon along with William Lambarde and William Somner. His great work had come to be admired as a phenomenon rather than read as a mere book, and criticism of it was frowned on by all but the most knowledgeable and sophisticated.

That at least was the comfortable state of affairs until the examination of half-a-dozen boxes of neglected manuscripts in the cathedral library at Canterbury resulted in the Hasted legend's being tested against the facts revealed by those manuscripts.

Chapter Two

THE IRBY DEPOSIT (1)

THE CATHEDRAL LIBRARY at Canterbury has a long and varied history. It is a direct successor of the old monastic library which must have been the first to be established in England; it even has some of the former monastic documents, which is a wonder when one reads of the way the monks' literary treasures were pillaged, not least by the archbishops. In Victorian times the Dean and Chapter found that their 17th-century library was becoming too small and built a new one amid the remains of the dormitory of the old priory. This received a direct hit during World War II from a large German bomb and it is amazing that the greater part of the contents survived. Whether this was due to the miraculous interposition of St Thomas of Canterbury or to more mundane causes we do not know, though it is worthy of mention that the bomb was high explosive and caused no fire; it penetrated through the building into the soft earth beneath. The foundations were thoroughly shaken and undermined, but the walls remained precariously erect for some hours before collapsing into a heap of rubble. Many of the valuable books had, in fact, been removed to safer storage in the Cathedral and those that remained were protected by extremely stout and solid bookcases.

When the time came to rebuild, the Pilgrim Trust generously supplemented the official war damage payments and the present splendid library resulted, built in a style described by a modern writer as 'Neo-Norman-cum-Tudoresque'. The Pilgrim Trust made it a condition that the historic collections should be available for scholars to study and the building is well-adapted and well-patronised for this purpose; whether or not due to the influence of the Pilgrim Trust, it is said to be modelled on the library of an American university. The air-conditioned strong room stores not only the documents of the cathedral, diocese and city, but also historically valuable collections lodged by their owners for safe keeping. One of the collections thus entrusted to the Dean and Chapter in the 1950s was an assortment of books and papers belonging to the Irby family. As would be expected, lists are kept of these deposits and the then cathedral archivist made a brief record of the contents of the deposit, noting that some of the papers were in the hand of Edward Hasted and concluding that Hasted had been 'collecting material after the publication of his *History*'. The Irby deposit was then boxed, lodged in the strong room and largely forgotten. The very few people who showed any interest in this archive consulted it not for its connection with Hasted, but for their own pet subjects, perhaps medieval history, perhaps Romano-British archaeology, about which it seems to have provided some meagre information. The casual enquirer interested in the historian of Kent would learn only of a rumour that the deposit included some of his letters, a document vaguely described as his 'Journal' and an account by him of the remains of a Roman temple discovered in central Canterbury.

Thus matters remained for some fifteen or twenty years during which important decisions concerning Hasted's *History* were taken by people who, so far as is known, had no interest in, or even knowledge of, the Irby deposit. It was resolved to reprint the *History*, and to take as the canon the second edition as being 'more reliable and convenient' and to precede it by a monograph on Hasted's life and his compiling of the book.

At Canterbury, in the meantime, a new cathedral and city archivist (Anne Oakley) had been appointed, and after surveying her new domain she had mentally resolved that, as soon as there was time, she would have a close look at the Irby deposit to find out precisely what it was. By the time the opportunity presented itself, the reprint of the *History* was an accomplished fact, and even then the archivist had to give up her plan of looking through the collection herself and allow the work to be done by proxy. An unpaid part-time volunteer worker in the library, engaged on the routine task of cataloguing 18th-century quarter-session records had asked for a change from the monotony of his work, if only as a temporary measure. This assistant was mildly interested in Hasted and his *History*, the second edition of which he had recently read, or perhaps skimmed through, from end to end; and when the archivist offered him the task of reporting on a collection which was reputed to contain some of the historian's letters he jumped at the chance. The archivist no doubt sighed as an enthusiast deprived of an interesting job, but consented, as a very busy administrator, to its being taken on by another. The unpaid part-time volunteer worker was, in fact, myself, and the rest of this book relates what I found in the Irby deposit, the remarkable conclusions drawn from its contents, the ramifications of those conclusions in other repositories in Kent and in London, and the further startling theories that resulted.

*   *   *

There were a dozen document boxes to search, all marked with the code reference 'U 11'. The contents of the boxes were very varied: one contained nothing but wax seals, but the bulk consisted of large books, loose papers, files of letters and two volumes of extracts from wills, labelled as such in Latin. There was a book of legal precedents, and one of kitchen recipes, a series of letters from an Oxford under-graduate to his father, William Boteler, many pedigrees, and a good deal of matter relating to the village of Eastry in East Kent, including what looked like census documents. Seven of the 12 boxes, however, seemed to concern Edward Hasted, and there were indeed 17 letters written and signed by him, addressed to William Boteler, which someone had filed in a docket. Many of them were lengthy; the first was written on 11 October 1795 and addressed to 'William Boteler, Esq. of Eastry, Kent' from 'St. George's Fields'. In addition to the many loose items, letters, memoranda, questionnaires and so forth, there were three large albums crammed with notes in Hasted's hand and an enormous collection of letters addressed to him, some loosely bound in book fashion and others unbound but stitched together. A paper-bound assemblage of miscellaneous writings was labelled 'Collections for the Hundreds of Bewsborough, Cornilo, Eastry and part of Ringlow'.

There were many indications that the Hasted manuscripts must be closely connected with his *History.* The letters addressed to him were endorsed with the names
of Kentish villages and towns, and the albums were predominantly devoted to notes
under similar local headings, the names of the places being arranged alphabetically.

I reported what I had found to the archivist and was instructed to examine and
report on the whole 'U 11' collection, concentrating especially on the Hasted
material. After the quarter sessions drudgery, this represented a welcome promotion
to more interesting work.

From a first look, the large albums and masses of letters seemed to be such a
close-textured mass of information that one could not expect to make anything
more detailed than a description of their general character without immense
research. The albums, especially, looked completely impervious to any brief perusal
with their masses of hieroglyphics, unintelligible abbreviations and sometimes illegible
writing, and their references to ancient books that with few exceptions one had
never even heard of. There were warnings of the erudition that would be needed
for the study of them in the form of references to the Great Roll of the Pipe, to the
King's Remembrancer, the Memoranda and Originalia; the Petty Bag Office; the Court
of Wards and the Star Chamber. The elucidation of a single page out of the many
hundreds would require prolonged study and probably considerable technical
knowledge. The predominant feeling of anyone but a trained and informed scholar
looking for the first time at this collection must be that of awe mixed with a certain
amount of amazement, and a feeling of being completely out of one's depth. The
huge batches of correspondence would no doubt be more readily intelligible, but
it would take a very long time to go through them all, and even longer to understand
and analyse their contents. The letters, though less technical and cryptic than the
albums, were in hundreds of different hands of varying decipherability. The loose
documents were a completely unknown quantity and in a state of the wildest
confusion; without taking a look at each one, little could be said about them
except that they were loose documents.

On the principle of taking first that part of the collection whose nature was the
least obvious, I decided to examine the loose documents first. Turning out the
contents of the relevant box I took the item that happened to be at the top of
the pile and examined it carefully. It was a short letter with a two-page questionnaire attached to it. The letter was in a sprawling hand with ample flourishes and
not too easy to read, even the signature, which I deciphered as 'C. J. Logan'. The
date was 6 April 1799, and this was the text:

> Sir,
>   I have made all the alterations that I know of according to your desire.
> The Maison Dieu Lands near Dover are Divided. I imagine Mr. Gunman
> hath the demesne lands; and the Lieut. Governor of Dover Castle for the
> time being the Farm; but how it came annexed to that office I never
> could learn.
>   I am Sir Yr Obdt. Servt.

The writing of the questionnaire was, from comparison with the letters signed by
him, clearly that of Edward Hasted. In form it was a list of manors and properties

in Dover and nearby parishes, giving the owners and residents in 1792 and asking about alterations and changes since; about a third of the queries were answered in the scrawling hand of 'Logan'; the rest unanswered, presumably to indicate no change. The date of the letter, 1799, and the year 1792 on which the questionnaire was based raised problems that had to remain unsolved for the moment.

The next obvious step was to see whether the text of the *History* gave any clue as to the purpose and use of the questionnaire. At that time I was working with the second edition, the one selected 'in collaboration with the Kent County Library' for reproduction, and generally available to the public. I had never even opened a copy of the first edition.

The Maison Dieu was an ancient medieval hospital, and its building now forms part of the Dover town hall. The Maison Dieu lands would perhaps be those that had once been part of the endowment of the hospital. In the account of Dover in the *History* there was a good deal about the Maison Dieu but nothing about the Maison Dieu lands. More helpfully, the list of vicars of St Mary's parish gave the incumbent as John *Lyon*. It was highly probable that it was his florid and flourish-adorned signature that looked like 'C. J. *Logan*'. Looking for an item in the questionnaire to which Lyon had given a positive answer, I selected the one concerning Wanson farm in the parish of St Margaret's-at-Cliffe. Hasted had written; 'The York family owners: query who?' and Lyon's answer was 'Lord Hardwick'. This parish comes in volume 9 of the second edition of the *History* published in 1800 and therefore after Hasted had received this answer, according to which (p. 413) the farm still belonged to the Yorks; however, in volume 10 there were Addenda to volume 9 and sure enough it was here recorded that 'Wanston [*sic*] Farm is now owned by the Earl of Hardwick'.

This was a turning point; the questionnaire was the actual and original source of the statement in the Addenda. This simple fact gave a new significance to the Irby manuscripts and, whatever the difficulties, they must be closely and thoroughly examined. The archivist agreed it would be important to find out whether the papers threw any light on Hasted's methods. Proceeding, then, I found that most of the other alterations Lyon reported could be traced either in the main text of the *History* or in the Addenda: as to why some had been immediately incorporated and others left for the Addenda was one more mystery.[1]

There were amongst the loose documents a number of even longer question-naires, and to avoid having to spend long periods immured in the cathedral library I had photocopies made so that I could take them away for further study. Two very strange-looking papers invited instant attention as a prelude to what might well develop into a long and laborious process. The first was a sheet of crude drawings with captions in an antique script in old French. There must originally have been six small designs. Two were drawn on pieces of transparent paper pinned to the sheet and one had been neatly cut out so that about a sixth of the paper was missing. The five that remained seemed to be symbolic representations of walled towns. Something in the design of the drawings struck a chord and a search through the Canterbury volumes of the *History* revealed (again in the Addenda—this time to volume 11) a plate with two similar designs. A note explained that this was taken from a manuscript of Matthew Paris's *History* 'written, as supposed, by himself about the middle of the thirteenth century. It is', says Hasted, 'a map of stations for a pilgrimage from England to the Holy Land consisting of rude drawings of all the towns en route'. That of Canterbury 'exhibits the Cathedral with three towers and without the walls of the city a church superscribed *"l'abbie Seie Augustin".'* There is then a reference to Figure I of the plate and that figure exactly supplied the missing part of Hasted's paper. Then we are told (in the *History*) that 'in the Benet College MSS. of the first part of the same author' there is a similar map where the towns are differently represented. In spite of there being no cross-reference this must refer to Figure II on the plate. One of the designs on Hasted's sheet was obviously a partial and incomplete version of Figure II.

Another note, written by Hasted and headed 'Gough's Topography p. 85' clearly referred to the drawings and, on my comparing it with the remarks about them quoted above, was found to coincide exactly. Surprisingly, Gough's *Topography* is in the cathedral library and turned out to be the source both of the diagrams and of the explanation of them. Yet Hasted made no acknowledgement of this borrowing.

The next document to catch the eye was written on a stiffish piece of paper which seemed to have been separated from another piece by a cut following a wavy line, after the manner of a medieval legal document known as a chirograph. This, however, was not a legal document but a letter, written in miniscule hand-writing, dated 4 November 1798 and signed 'W. Boteler'. Moreover, it was a complete letter, no part having been cut away, and was in effect in the form of a right-angled triangle with a wavy hypotenuse. Another curious fact was that the straight sides of the letter were bordered by a thick black line and a thinner parallel line. Moreover down the wavy side could be seen here and there some faint printed lines roughly parallel to the edge. It took quite some time to reach what should perhaps have been the obvious conclusion, that the letter was written on part of a map which had a vacant space in the corner representing sea. It was then easy to identify the map as that of the Hundreds of Cornilo and Bewsborough, shown opposite p. 375 in volume 9 of the *History*. The letter, in fact, refers to the map which the writer describes as 'very erroneous'. He had done his best to correct it but was still far from satisfied with it but hoped that with the corrections it gave 'a tolerable idea of the whole'.[2]

Even more striking, in matter if not in form, were three letters from Boteler evidently sent after the publication of volumes 9 and 10 of the second edition, which related to the area where he lived. Great lists of errors are pointed out and in many cases Boteler complains that he is drawing attention to them for the second time. Even worse is one instance where Boteler himself has supplied information which has appeared correctly in the first edition, but which has been changed, resulting in an incorrect second edition. And Boteler was not the only critic. Several other correspondents sent letters, often with lengthy schedules listing the errors they had found in the later volumes of the second edition. About 80 per cent. of the Corrigenda of volumes 9 and 10 are attributable to these commentators. There were besides many letters from eminent people. Sir Samuel Egerton-Brydges, whom we have already met, wrote voluminously and supplied details from time to time of his latest property acquisitions; other correspondents were William Deedes,

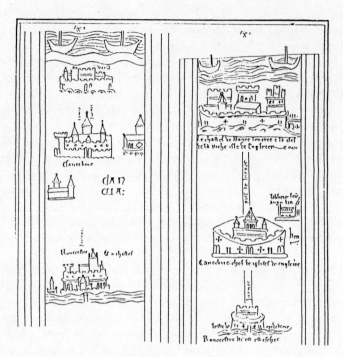

Fig. 1.

Fig. 2.

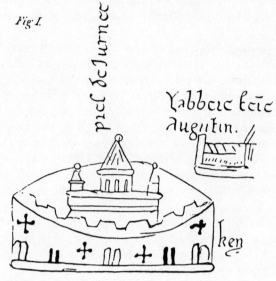

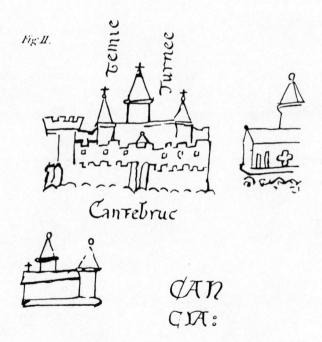

Fig. 3.

Figs. 1, 2 and 3. An unacknowledged borrowing. Fig. 1 is
from Gough's *Topography* (1768); Fig. 2 is Hasted's copy
of it, with a piece excised; Fig. 3 is the resulting print appearing in Hasted's *History*.

ancestor of the present editor of the *Daily Telegraph,* William Boys, the historian of Sandwich, and Henry Godfrey Faussett, son of the famous Kent archaeologist, Bryan Faussett.

It would be tedious to particularise the confused mass of press-cuttings, church inscriptions, letters and questionnaires, about plates, maps and current affairs, amounting to 92 items all told. There was a draft of the dedication of the fourth volume of the first edition to William Pitt, and a pedigree of the posterity of John Evelyn, the celebrated diarist and writer on philosophy and horticulture. 'I had this account', Hasted had written, 'from Hugh E. presumptive heir to Sir Frederick Evelyn, his second cousin—in 1798 a prisoner in the King's Bench Prison and partly deranged'. This gives support perhaps to Dr. Johnson's observation that 'no man will be a sailor who has contrivance enough to get himself into a jail, where he will have . . . commonly better company'. The pedigree shows that Halsted's fellow-prisoner was the great-grandson of the diarist.

By now it was becoming clear that the seven 'Hasted boxes' of deposit U 11 contained some of Hasted's most important working papers and, without jumping to conclusions, more and more probable that these were the papers left to William Boteler in the codicil to Hasted's will.[3]

Chapter Three

THE IRBY DEPOSIT (2)

BEFORE STARTING on the next stage of the inspection of the documents it seemed to be essential, both for clarity and completeness, to find out what exactly were the differences between the first and second editions of the *History*. Work had started on the footing that Hasted's *History of Kent* meant the second edition—the one that was to be found in the public libraries in its newly reprinted form, and which had, by implication, the imprimatur of the Kentish historical establishment.

A line-by-line comparison of the whole of the two editions was obviously out of the question, but the study of a few specimen parishes would give a rough idea of what had happened; accordingly a start was made with Hougham and North-bourne in east Kent. By using photocopies and marking the alterations made for the second edition it was discovered that the second edition was, overall, an abridgement of the first, and that the excisions were much greater than one had been led to expect from any published account. The parochial articles were rearranged as well; the topographical descriptions, relegated to the end of the accounts in the first edition, now came near the beginning, and were fuller and much more readable. The first edition was noteworthy for the number and length of its footnotes, which on some pages occupied more space than the parent text. This was all changed; if the substance of the notes was retained it was inserted into the main text, and there was only an occasional footnote, usually of an authority. There seemed to be certain standard practices of economy, such as omitting the original text of Domesday entries and leaving only the English translations of them. Again, the lists of incumbents of the churches were usually reduced by deleting all names prior to about 1660, a somewhat strange expedient. In the first edition it was Hasted's practice to give very full information about the authorities from which he derived his statements, but most of this was omitted in the second edition. One could not help receiving the impression that a few authorities had been left in here and there for the sake of appearance. The work had been done, on the whole, with admirable skill. Legal flummery and superfluous descriptions were ruthlessly cut, and a host of sidelines which, though interesting, were not necessary to the main narrative, were excised. In particular the ramifications of the histories of the different families were cut out if they did not affect the descent of the family estates. By these methods the historical matter had been cut by about one-third. The job was done in such a crisp and businesslike manner that I remarked to the archivist that Hasted would have made an excellent newspaper sub-editor. But this discovery presented a problem: to use the second edition alone, assuming that the first would be approximately similar, was no longer justified, and it seemed essential to acquire a copy of the first for my own use when outside the cathedral library.

A set of the first (folio) edition of Hasted's *Kent* is a much valued possession and (unlike the second edition) this issue has not been reprinted; as much as £1,200 has been given in the saleroom for a specially prized set. However, I managed to secure cheaply four volumes that had been stripped of maps and engravings but were otherwise intact.

The constant repetition of the expressions 'first edition' and 'second edition' becomes tedious. The abbreviations 'F' (folio) for the first and 'O' (octavo) for the second are used in my notes, and, with the reader's approval, will be employed from time to time in these pages. The volumes can also be labelled F I, II, II and IV, and O 1, 2, 3, etc.

The loose documents having been disposed of (except for various odd pieces of written matter which continued to turn up inside the covers of albums and portfolios interleaved in or lying hidden beneath them in the bottom of document boxes) it was necessary to plan the next move. Besides the loose papers and the docketed letters from Hasted there were the following groups of manuscripts to choose from: two volumes of will extracts, two large portfolios of correspondence, three albums of notes, the paper-bound *Collections for the Hundreds of Bewsborough, Cornilo, &c.,* and another stitched-together bundle of letters and memoranda, the nature of which was a complete mystery since it had no cover or binding nor any indication whatever as to its subject-matter.

It seemed to be a good idea to tackle next the last two, the *Collections,* because they looked easier and more straightforward than some of the other material, and would yield the most information for the least effort, and the anonymous package because it seemed rather desirable to obtain at least a clue as to what it was.

Taking the *Collections* first, apart from a small amount of correspondence (mostly between Hasted and Boteler), the 194 pages comprised a closely-written mass of information arranged by parishes within the Hundreds of the title which comprise the extreme eastern part of the county. It seemed that this information had been prepared to enable Hasted, then exiled in Calais, to complete his writing of the fourth and last volume of the *History.* Most of this literary pabulum was shipped across the Channel in 1792, with just a few items sent in the early months of the following year. The significance of these dates was obvious and explains why, when updating his information in 1799, Hasted was concerned to know what had occurred since 1792. There was a list of 51 properties about which Hasted presumably required information, though these are by no means all of those which figured in his account of the named Hundreds. If Hasted did, in fact, give Boys and Boteler a precise remit as to what information he needed it has been lost, but between them the two partners supplied general descriptions of the parishes, topography, soils, cultivation, etc., and reported who were the present owners of the most important properties, manors and seats, with a sketch of the recent descent of each property where known. They supplied a very full picture of the parish government, detailing the 'boroughs' (rural wards), manors and courts which had the privilege of appointing the parish constables and borsholders, and the territorial jurisdiction of the various manors. The work done most systematically was in relation to the churches. For every parish church they provided a brief description of the structure, followed by a complete and detailed list of the monuments and inscriptions inside it and of those in the churchyard in so far as they were decipherable. The two enthusiasts seem to have taken on an approximately equal share of the fieldwork, but Boteler seems to have handled most of the correspondence with Hasted. Comparing the Boteler/Boys productions with the text of Volume IV of the first edition one noticed some interesting facts. The use that Hasted made of the information was quite plain because it was very much his habit to simply copy out almost word by word what was supplied to him and insert it into his *History*. This gave a very clear picture of Hasted as a 'scissors and paste' man, simply assembling the facts, making little attempt to make any synthesis of his own from them, but merely repeating whatever he was supplied with; thus revealed, his debt to Boteler and Boys was very substantial.

Hasted's treatment of the little village of Eythorne, near Dover, throws some interesting sidelights on his methods. Item 9 of the list of properties on which he wanted information reads: 'Eythorne manor owned in 1660 by Brett; 1760 by Sherbrooke'. To this Boteler had answered: 'The estate passed from Richard Sherbrook [*sic*] to his sister who marrying — Mead by her had issue a daughter who marrying John Wilkes Esq. carried it to this family, his only daughter Mary being the present possessor'.

Hasted's account follows Boteler's information in practically the same words and typically neither thought it worth mentioning that Wilkes was one of the leading political figures of his time, that he had been Lord Mayor of London and that his daughter was the famous Polly Wilkes who acted as her father's Lady Mayoress, and whose correspondence with her father can be seen in the British Library. Boteler gave a description of Polly Wilkes' manor house, observing that the walls 'are much covered with ivy the stems of which are the strongest I ever saw'. Printing these words verbatim Hasted gives the untrue impression that he himself had observed the ivy. Almost half of the text relating to Eythorne comes from Boteler's information.

Between two of the pages of the *Collections* was found a letter to William Boteler from a Mr. J. S. Harvey of Tilmanstone, asking that 'the errors in Hasted's former volumes respecting the arms borne by our family' be corrected in the one forthcoming. The only feature of this letter worth remembering is the name of the writer, J. S. Harvey. We shall be hearing a good deal more about him later on.

So much for the *Collections for Bewsborough, etc.*; now for the unbound bundle of correspondence. It started with a letter addressed by Boteler to Simmons, the printer, followed by Simmons' reply. Boteler, writing on 7 August 1790, asks Simmons whether he can supply a copy of the map of Kent 'that accompanies Mr. Hasted's *History*'. He also offers to correct the maps of certain Hundreds in which he had observed mistakes, and begs Simmons not to print the map of Eastry, Boteler's home ground, until Boys and he had seen it 'for I hear you mean to continue the work'. This is very significant; it can only be a reference to Hasted's flight to France, for what else could have put the continuation of Simmons' work in jeopardy? If this supposition is correct, Hasted must have gone abroad as early as 1790, not 1791 as he himself records in the list of the events of his life—an amazing example of his tendency to inaccuracy.[1] Boteler then continues:

> Many little errors have crept into Mr. Hasted's work which I am sorry to see, as they might have been corrected if he had made use of his friends in a proper manner. But it was his custom to solicit information and in the meantime print off the subject he was inquiring after before he could receive it, at least this is the conduct he preserved towards me.

Simmons' reply is perhaps worth setting out in full, if only because this is the only letter from him that we seem to have:

> It is out of my power at present to oblige you with a map of the county, and Mr. Hasted purported to have some alterations made on the plate before he had any more impressions taken off. I think it likely that I may receive some orders respecting thereto, and whenever any more impressions are taken from it I will certainly procure one for you. Your remarks on Mr. Hasted's conduct are too true; in numberless instances he might have made his work much more correct, but he was frequently too late in making application to his friends, and having made it, much too precipitate in printing off his sheets without waiting for it.
>
> The fate of the fourth volume is yet undetermined but should I have any principal concern therein I shall be most happy in the assistance of yourself and Mr. Boys.
>
> The return of Mr. Hasted is very uncertain but he has much material with him that were they digested and methodically transcribed I should not despair of procuring such essential help as would render the fourth at least equal to the preceding volumes, but what may be the event it is at present impossible to forecast.
>
> I have no single numbers of the Gents' Magazine.

After a good deal of puzzlement and perplexity I concluded that the Boteler-Simmons exchange had nothing to do with the rest of the bundle but was quite extraneous. The remainder of the letters, etc., were themselves something of a mixture, starting off with a solid mass of 55 pages, in John Lyon's scrawl, relating to Dover and parishes in its neighbourhood. This was parallel to the contributions of Boys and Boteler contained in the *Collections for Bewsborough, &c.*; between them Lyon's 'screed' and Boteler's *Collections* covered the coastline from west of Dover up to and including the isle of Thanet.

After Lyon's 55 pages came a disordered series of letters received from many persons over many years, with some more recent ones from the old firm of Boys and Boteler which might just as well have been included in the *Collections for Bewsborough, &c.* Interspersed were sheets of Hasted's own notes. All the letters and notes relate to the east Kent region or to the city of Canterbury—the localities described in Hasted's fourth and last folio volume.[2]

Some of the letters from Boys throw a significant light on Hasted's personal circumstances or on his methods. Like Boteler, Boys, too, is clamouring for the chance to see the proofs before the accounts of the places in which he is interested are printed. He is concerned also for Hasted's health; writing in March 1790 from Sandwich, he concludes:

> Your indisposition, most likely, is the consequence of your long confinement. Change the air and use exercise and all will be right again. I would recommend the air of Sandwich to you in the summer and some of the pigs and poultry of Statenborow and Goshall by way of restorative. We shall have quantum sufficient for the broods are already numerous and forward.

This is one of several references to be found in Hasted's correspondence to his illness in 1790, which he himself attributed to the after-effects of some dreadful accident he had sustained on one of his information-gathering trips about Kent. There is no account of this accident, so far as can be ascertained, in the local press, and the thought occurs (not too uncharitably one hopes) that perhaps the accident and following illness were 'diplomatic'. Hasted was heavily in debt, and by inference in daily risk of arrest. This could be avoided by keeping to his house.

In a letter of 21 November 1791 Boys gives us another sidelight on Hasted's affairs, the sale of his books:

> I acted by advice in treating with your son for your books. There were some of them which I wished much to have; but I shall be better pleased to hear you have parted with them for a sum near your estimate of their value than to have had them fall into my hands at mine.

The next year (June 1792) Boys tried (vainly as it turned out) to suppress an erroneous passage in Hasted's account of Sandwich. Basing himself on Leland and Camden, Hasted had described how the sinking of 'a great ship of Pope Paul IV' had had 'a fatal effect towards the decay of the haven'. However, Boys, the official historian of Sandwich, writes: 'There is nothing known here of Pope Paul's ship. It could not possibly have occasioned any material injury to our haven by being wrecked at its mouth'.

But this was like pouring water on a duck's back so far as the historian of Kent was concerned, and the story can still be read in both the first and second editions. Boys had somewhat better success in correcting Hasted's dramatic account (copied word by word from Lewis's *Thanet,* without acknowledgement) of the manner in which a ship striking the Goodwin Sands was swallowed whole by the quicksands 'so that no part of it would be left to be seen'. Boys' contrary opinion, that the sands were as firm as those of Sandwich Bay and that the ships were destroyed by being broken to pieces by the action of the waves, Hasted condescended to mention in a footnote, while retaining in the text the account which Boys, who must have landed on the sands or taken his facts from someone else who had done so, considered to be quite false.

We can now revert to Lyon's notes which, in the strange business of the inscribed Roman tile found at Dover, provide an interesting example of valuable information being jettisoned in Hasted's second edition. Every student of Romano-British archaeology knows of the *Classis Britannica* (British Fleet)

Fig. 4. The printer's proof of p. 689 of Volume III of the Folio edition. Most of the extensive amendments are probably in the hand of William Boys.

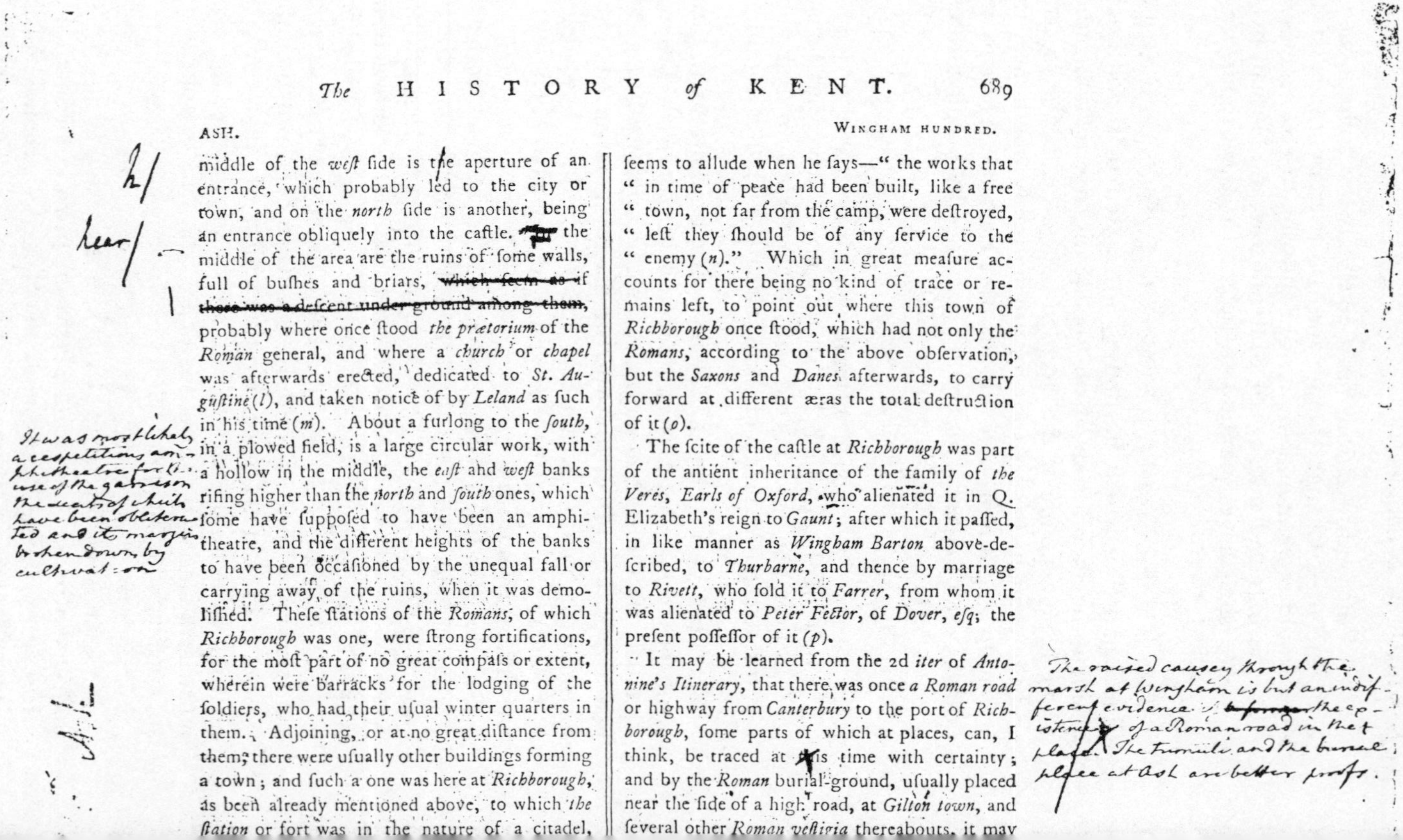

The H I S T O R Y of K E N T. 689

WINGHAM HUNDRED.

ASH.

middle of the *weft* fide is *the* aperture of an entrance, which probably led to the city or town, and on the *north* fide is another, being an entrance obliquely into the caftle, *as* the middle of the area are the ruins of fome walls, full of bufhes and briars, ~~which form is of there was defcent under ground among them~~, probably where once ftood *the prætorium* of the *Roman* general, and where a *church* or *chapel* was afterwards erected, dedicated to *St. Auguftine*(*l*), and taken notice of by *Leland* as fuch in his time (*m*). About a furlong to the *fouth*, in a plowed field, is a large circular work, with a hollow in the middle, the *eaft* and *weft* banks rifing higher than the *north* and *fouth* ones, which fome have fuppofed to have been an amphitheatre, and the different heights of the banks to have been occafioned by the unequal fall or carrying away, of the ruins, when it was demolifhed. Thefe ftations of the *Romans*, of which *Richborough* was one, were ftrong fortifications, for the moft part of no great compafs or extent, wherein were barracks for the lodging of the foldiers, who had, their ufual winter quarters in them. Adjoining, or at no great diftance from them, there were ufually other buildings forming a town, and fuch a one was here at *Richborough*, as been already mentioned above, to which *the ftation* or fort was in the nature of a citadel,

feems to allude when he fays——" the works that " in time of peace had been built, like a free " town, not far from the camp, were deftroyed, " left they fhould be of any fervice to the " enemy (*n*)." Which in great meafure accounts for there being no kind of trace or remains left, to point out, where this town of *Richborough* once ftood, which had not only the *Romans*, according to the above obfervation, but the *Saxons* and *Danes* afterwards, to carry forward at different æras the total deftruction of it (*o*).

The fcite of the caftle at *Richborough* was part of the antient inheritance of the family of *the Veres, Earls of Oxford*, who alienated it in Q. *Elizabeth's* reign to *Gaunt*; after which it paffed, in like manner as *Wingham Barton* above-defcribed, to *Thurbarne*, and thence by marriage to *Revett*, who fold it to *Farrer*, from whom it was alienated to *Peter Feftor*, of *Dover*, efq; the prefent poffeffor of it (*p*).

It may be learned from the 2d *iter* of *Anto- nine's Itinerary*, that there was once a *Roman* road or highway from *Canterbury* to the port of *Rich- borough*, fome parts of which at places, can, I think, be traced at this time with certainty; and by the *Roman* burial ground, ufually placed near the fide of a high road, at *Gilton town*, and feveral other *Roman veftiria* thereabouts, it may anno 1509, defired to this chapel of *Richborough*, to the ufe of it, &c. to make them a new window in the body of the church. It appears to have been *a chapel of eafe* to the church of *Afh*, for the few remaining inhabitants of this diftrict, and is mentioned as fuch in the grant of the rectory of that church, anno 3 *Edward* VI. at which it appears to have exifted, but I find no mention whatever made of it afterwards, fo that moft probably it foon after fell to decay, and the fite of it is now only known by the above defcription of *Leland*.

(m) The walls of the caftle are built of various materials; the infide of chalk-rubble and flints, the outfides are faced with rows of .... ftone, ..., and laid throughout at every three feet four inches with two courfes of *Roman* tiles, 16 .... turned up at the ends thus:

.... fo as being laid tranfverfely to clafp into each other, and form a ftrong bandage to the reft of the wall. The *fouth* and *eaft* corner of the wall is entirely down for about a rod and an half. The *north* fide is moft entire, the entrance, at which, the *porta decumana*, is very fair, to the *weft* of which, in the fame wall, there appears, about three or four rods from it, to have been a hollow fpace for a build-ing, about fix feet deep and 12 long; perhaps for the watch-tower of the caftle. About three rods eaftward of the above entrance, there is an oblong fquare ftone, fomewhat protu-berant, about three parts in the height of the wall, no doubt once the head of *St. Bertha*, as defcribed by *Leland*. Quan-tities of *Roman* coins have been continually found over the whole furface of this area, and at the *north-eaft* corner of it, great numbers of boars tufks, and flags antlers fawed off, and oyfter-fhells; and the hufbandmen note, that when their

from the reft of it. In the middle is the ground called *St. Auguftine's crofs*, now even with the foil and grown over with bufhes. ...., there was within thefe few years a plat-form of fquare tiles, leading towards the river, dug up.—The ground mentioned by *Leland*, as between *Richborough* and *Sandwich*, with a dike caft up round it, called *Little-borough*, is by fome fuppofed to have been raifed by the *Danes* fo late as the year 990, when they made themfelves mafters of this caftle.

(n) See Horfley's Brit. p. 101.

(o) The burial-ground for this *Roman* colony and ftation of *Richborough*, appears to have been on the broad hill of fand on the *fouth* fide of the *eaft* end of *Gilton town*, in *Afh* parish, about two miles *fouth-weft* from the caftle. The many graves which have been continually dug up, there, in different parts of it, fhew it to have been of general ufe for that purpofe for feveral ages. .... hardly po-ffible to move any part of the earth, without finding a grave, and different forts of *Roman* remains depofited within them. Thefe have been from time to time preferved in the col-lections of the curious and learned in the neighbourhood. Mr. *Fauffet*, of *Heppington*, has many valuable *Roman* re-mains, dug up by his father at this place. Mr. *Boys*, of *Sandwich*, has feveral of them, moft of which he has caufed to be engraved.

(p) In the deed of conveyance it is thus defcribed :— And alfo all thofe the walls and ruins of the antient caftle of *Rutupium*, now known by the name of *Richborough* caftle, with the fcite of the antient port and city of *Rutupinum*, being on and near the lands above-mentioned. About the walls of *Richborough* grows *Fænfculum vulgare*, common fennel, in great plenty.

Vol. III. 8 N

	Baptony Births	Marriages	Averages	
1910 to 1719	149	—	119	70
20 to 29	121	—	99	65
30 to 39	155	—	101	22
40 to 49	150	—	93	37
50 to 59	145	—	100	52
60 to 69	125	—	128	35
70 to 75	140	—	124	

which the Romans organised to guard the Channel and nearby coasts. Its bases were at Boulogne and Dover, and for the construction of its shore installations it evidently maintained its own brickworks, the products being marked with the letters CL BR for *Classis Britannica.* It is very interesting to read, in a 33-page memorandum that John Lyon sent to Hasted in 1792, an account of the finding of a tile so inscribed at St Mary's church in Dover, of which Lyon was the minister. The west end of the church, Lyon says, was built upon the ruins of a Roman bath-house. He gives a very detailed description of the hypocaust, or heating-chamber, including the dimensions of the *pylae*—brick columns supporting the floor of the hot-room above it—and then refers to the tile and attempts to reproduce the lettering; this he interprets as C I BR, which he says may be read *Cohors Prima Britannica,* a reference (Lyon thinks) to the first cohort of the Second Legion which latter was, in the later period of the Roman occupation, stationed on this coast. It was not until the 1850s that the famous antiquary, Charles Roach Smith, established the true meaning of the CL BR stamps on the tiles.

Anyone reading the second edition will find no mention of the tile but only a bald statement that Lyon had discovered the remains of a Roman structure 'which he apprehended to have been a bath, at the west end of the parish church of St Mary'. If such a reader had later come across Lyon's letter he would deduce that Hasted was injudicious in his selection of facts to print. But if the reader should then refer to the first edition he would find Lyon's account set out virtually complete. Anyone relying on the second edition only would thus be deprived of all knowledge of a most interesting and significant fact.

Chapter Four

THE HASTED/BOTELER CORRESPONDENCE

THE DISCOVERY of so many letters from Boteler was now beginning to give a new significance to the 17 docketed letters of Hasted. It was hoped that married together, and supplemented by the extra letters bound up in the *Collections* and elsewhere, an interesting two-way correspondence could be built up. All the letters were therefore photocopied, as it is not permissible to detach and rearrange documents in a repository. The copies were then arranged in chronological order and the result was highly satisfactory; there were now 20 Hasted letters and an equal number of Boteler's, the earliest letter written by Boteler on 27 March 1790, and the last one by Hasted on 24 November 1803.[1] The sequence was—not unexpectedly—incomplete: there were two gaps of over a year and to all intents and purposes the correspondence ended with the publication of the last volume of the second edition of the *History,* the two letters (one each way) in 1803 forming no part of the main stream. Yet the overall effect is that of reasonable continuity.

The correspondence begins with Boteler writing to Hasted when the historian was still in England but shortly before the start of his voluntary exile in France:

Eastry
27th March 1790

Dear Sir,

I received your favour of the 25th and am glad to hear you are so advanced in the progress of your History. I have not got on so fast as I could wish in my efforts to assist owing to many causes, and unfortunately my enquiries have been directed to places I find you have finished with. Sir Br. Bridges had been so obliging as to give me what information he could respecting his several estates the greater part of which some proof sheets of your work inform me I might have spared my labour about. I was led to take that district as being the nearest to you and most likely to be first wanted; I could have wished it had not been so as I could have noticed some things you have omitted and corrected some little mistakes.

I send with this what I have collected relative to Betshanger and Northbourne as a specimen only of what I mean to glean in every place as far as I can; when you have read it you may if you please return it with observations and if I have omitted anything necessary for your information within my power, minute it down.

Would you wish me to particularize the names of the persons on the Church Monuments and to provide a list of the rectors and vicars from the Registers? The charities in each parish I conclude you have an account

of and I do not meddle with the more ancient history as I suppose you
are already acquainted with that. In short arrange for me systematically
every point of enquiry, and if you will give me a few places in the order
you next want them I by that means can allow a little more time to each
and yet keep before you. You must excuse the desultory manner I have
used in my collections; I mean it as a jumble of notes to be understood
only.

Boteler then rambles off into detail about a place-name before coming to a
criticism of Hasted's description of the village of Ash which was included in the
third volume just about to be published, but of which Boteler had evidently seen
the proofs:

I have most carefully read your account of Ash and am much pleased
with it, but could have wished to have seen it whilst alteration was
possible. I am sure you will excuse me for saying this as from the nature
of the work the wonder is that there should be so few mistakes creep in.
Your account of the population as taken from the register I hope does not
stand as it is an error of the 1st magnitude. Promise me only, my dear Sir,
that Eastry, and every contiguous Parish to it, shall not be finally done till
Boys and I have seen them. Don't censure my presumption in making
this request; locality will give you opportunities for information that
cannot be procured at a distance.

Again Boteler goes off in other detail before concluding:

If I knew when you might be found at home I think I would steal over
and pass a long day with you.
                         Believe me with great truth Dear Sir,
                                   Yours most faithfully,
                                   W. BOTELER

The information about Betteshanger and Northbourne would be for the purpose
of the fourth volume which Hasted, in spite of his difficulties, intended to proceed
with immediately. But why was Boteler collecting the information even before
Hasted's flight to France? If we assume that Hasted had already realised that he
might have to flee, it is unlikely that he could tell Boteler this for the whole object of
Hasted's manoeuvering would be secrecy; moreover, Boteler was in almost daily
contact with William Boys, and there are letters from him which reveal no inkling
of Hasted's intentions. This was an addition to the growing list of questions to
which no answer could be given at this stage.

It is nearly two years before we have another letter, in February 1792. This
covers the despatch to Hasted, now established in Calais, of the fruits of Boteler's
researches in seven East Kent parishes:

No person wishes more heartily to assist the Business than myself;
why I have not done more I think I can satisfactorily explain. In the first
place I do not like to apply thro' others for information; at least am not
satisfied without being on the spot myself and sifting by a cross examination; for the ignoramuses, if you will allow the word, that we must get

information from generally mistake the tenor of two questions out of three; at least, I have often found, like Dr. Johnson in the Highlands, that the answer to the second has frequently nullified the first. To steer clear of error is my first desire, and I trust, by the samples I have sent you, it will not be found that I have skimmed the surface only; now Sir that I might not be obliged to be continually deserting the object in view I had reserved the month of September for the purpose, as at that time Mr. Boys had promised me the assistance of his son Edward in my profession.

Boteler, William Boys and Boys' son, Edward, were all medical men. Unfortunately, however, as Boteler goes on to relate, no sooner had Boys junr. arrived to help him than Boteler himself 'was seized by a severe complaint that confined me to my House for three weeks . . . the weather being now better and the days coming longer I hope soon to complete the business'. Boteler hopes that he will 'in a very little time give you a better opinion of my diligence'.

In his reply from Calais, dated 10 March 1792, Hasted is lavish in his grateful thanks for the accurate information that Boteler had supplied, and takes up the comments about the ignoramuses of East Kent:

> I am very sentitive of the many difficulties you meet with in obtaining any accurate knowledge in your enquiries. It is what I have too often met with myself in my parochial progresses and in leaving a place I have frequently remained in greater doubt and uncertainties than when I entered it. But this is no more than must be expected from the universal ignorance prevailing among those who are alone left for us to make our enquiries of, and indeed from the total inattention so prevalent of everything which is not closely connected with—What shall I get by it—but I see by what you have sent me that your perseverance gets the better of all these difficulties.

To demonstrate that his confidence in Boteler's reliability is no mere expression of politeness Hasted sends several further questions relating to Eastry Hundred for Boteler's attention. We know now that the fourth folio volume on which Hasted was then busy was not to be published for another seven years and the next passage in the letter shows what a great disappointment this long delay must have been:

> May I trespass so far on you as to intreat the return of your endeavours for me before the end of May, for they will take me up much time afterwards to insert among my account, already in some measure drawn up, of the several parishes and I hope to get to Press by the beginning of July. If you would favour me with part of them, as you finish them, I should be much obliged to you as I can then be still jogging on to the end of my thirty years journey. I have drawn up as far as I can all but the Isle of Thanet and indeed some parishes in that too so that I hope I shall soon direct my pen to that line, that long wished for adage of *Deus dedit huic quoque finem.* (God gave an end to this also.)

And so Hasted's letter runs on. He wants sketches of some ancient fortifications near Coldred; he wants the continuance of Boys' assistance; he wants Boteler to help him recover a small sum of interest, accidentally left in the funds from more prosperous times, and ends with more profuse apologies and thanks.

In July Boteler sends some material for Hasted to be going on with and promises more soon. He also tells his friend how to proceed to obtain the small sum in the funds. Nevertheless, in his next letter, 19 August 1792, Hasted is still pressing Boteler for action: 'I am sorry I am forced to be so importunate with you for the dispatch of them but I am engaged to deliver up the MS. of my next volume to Mr. Simmons in the beginning of next month'. Feeling perhaps a little guilty over the way he is harrying Boteler Hasted offers him a collection of seals of noblemen and gentry which are among the belongings left at Canterbury.

On 12 December Boteler sends the last batch of information he has promised and explains the delay:

> The business, ever since your last pressing letter, has hung upon my mind as a dead weight; and it has been a matter of infinite regret to me that avocations of a much more disagreeable nature have prevented me from using a diligence that would have gratified my own inclinations in a favorite pursuit and have answered your wishes at the same time. I will not tire you with explanations that cannot mend the matter; suffice it to say that, altho' I have quitted the profession I was bred to, my time has been in a much greater degree arrested in fitting out my vessel for other ventures. Figure apart, I am become Farmer, Grazier, Hop planter and Hop merchant too.

Boteler was extremely proud of his family pedigree which he could trace with certainty back as far as the reign of Henry VI, but his family traditions insisted on their descent from one Richard or Robert de Boteler who lived in the time of Edward I. This is what Hasted intended to put in the *History,* but Boteler agonised and theorised about what he feared was a mere conjectural piece of family history. These doubts, however, do not seem to have worried the intrepid Hasted who printed as fact the family traditions that Boteler himself regarded as only presumptive and conjectural.

On 22 January 1793 Hasted again expressed his warm thanks for Boteler's assistance: 'Without yourself and my good friend Mr. Boys I should, and I am happy to acknowledge it, have fallen far short in my endeavours to finish it in any shape equal to the expectation of the Public or my own satisfaction'.

However, he adds 'There are 2 or 3 matters which I should be much obliged to you to satisfy me in, and that at the earliest opportunity you can, suitable to your own convenience'.

Then follows a series of intricate conundrums regarding the mystery of the Crayford and Morrice families. In Boteler's reply we see an example of research in action. Hasted has a 'communication' according to which Admiral Salmon Morrice of Betteshanger had disinherited the elder of his two sons, Wright Morrice. Not so, replies Boteler:

> As Wright Morrice died before his father I should apprehend you are misinformed with respect to his being disinherited. I have always heard from my family that his Brother William, or as they used ironically to

call him *Wrong* Morrice, was by far the cleverest fellow of the two and
the greatest favourite with his father, but never understood that Wright
was upon very ill terms with him.

This pleasant distinction between Wright and 'Wrong' Morrice may stay in the
mind because the Morrice family will crop up later in this investigation.

The next letter, bearing the date 20 December 1794, is different from all the
others in that strictly speaking it is one from William Boys to Hasted endorsed in
a much longer letter from Boteler to Boys. The latter had apparently received
from Hasted queries concerning the sale in lots of the Northbourne Court estate
which he had promptly passed on to Boteler. 'I can add nothing to it', says Boys,
referring to Boteler's answer. The letter is also unique in that it was sent in the
interregnum between Hasted's return to England (because of the outbreak of war)
and his arrest and incarceration in the debtors' prison. During this time he was
wandering about the country with Mary Jane Town hoping to escape notice. It
would be interesting, therefore, to know to what address this letter was sent, but,
unfortunately, there is no indication.

There is a gap of 10 months before the next letter of Hasted which reads as
follows:

> My good Sir,
>   I cannot omit an hour to throw myself on your goodness to pardon my
> strange behaviour to you today, but the sudden surprise, totally, as you
> might well see, deprived me of all recollection, not only of yourself
> but of whatever I might and ought to have mentioned to you; it deprived
> me of expressing the sincere and grateful sentiments of my heart for the
> many offers of friendship I have so often experienced from you, especially
> the last of late, at a time when I stood so much in want of it; believe me,
> the sudden effect my surprise of this day has had on me is such that
> I have not yet recovered it. I seem as in a dream [not] yet returned
> to my cool reason again. My dear sir, impute it not to ingratitude, I
> beseech you, impute it not to a designed behaviour and thus not having
> a due sense of the favor you did me and the pleasure it would have given
> me had not the surprise totally deprive me of expressing my feelings of it.
> Would you add to your former kindness by still conferring on me one
> further boon, that of taking the trouble of calling on me *again,* before you
> leave Town. I hope you will favor me in it. Indeed it will be a charity
> to ease me of these unpleasant sensations which now give me pain when I
> think of what has passed this day. I have besides some particular things
> which I wish much to speak to you on, on literary matters relating to
> my MSS. which I cannot communicate by letter. Oblige me in this favor
> my dear sir, to your already much obliged humble servant
>
> St George's Fields   EDWARD HASTED.
> Oct. 11th, 1795

It was at St George's Fields in Southwark that the King's Bench Debtors' Prison
was established. Both the inmates and people writing to them had some delicacy
at calling the place by its real name. Some letters addressed to Hasted during this
time at 'King's College, London', raised a doubt as to whether perhaps there was

some mistake and he had not been imprisoned at that time. This was quickly put at rest by a letter to the Public Record Office who confirmed the dates of his incarceration, and by the discovery of an entry in the *Dictionary of Phrase and Fable* which revealed an 18th-century practice of referring to prisons as 'colleges'. Newgate, for instance, was called 'New College' and the grim significance of the expression 'to pass one's final at New College' can easily be guessed. The letter is a surprising revelation of Hasted's emotional and almost neurotic nature and his unbelievable folly in quarrelling with those upon whom he depended, by his own account, for the materials for completing his *History,* and even from time to time for the money to keep him from starvation.

The next letter that we have, again from Hasted, is dated 1 December and is a reply to one from Boteler which is lost. Clearly Hasted's tearful appeal had had the desired effect:

> I received your last favor with much pleasure and thank you for every part of the contents of it. The satisfaction I feel at your assuring me that you pardon my late behaviour, however really unintentional, is far beyond my words to express to you and I earnestly entreat you that you will condescend to favor me when next you come to Town with a call on me here *once more,* that by my grateful reception of you I may convince you of the sincerity of my professions to you.

This little difficulty being satisfactorily overcome Hasted swiftly turns to business —the exact size of a vignette of Eastry church to be printed. He then accepts with alacrity Boteler's offer of further help:

> Your kind offer of assistance in future communications I shall gladly accept of, for within these 3 years, to which times your last kind informa- tions reached, there must have happened many alterations and changes. I am assured the work will go to press within the present month and that early in it and that it will go on without intermission. I sincerely hope it will for more reasons than that concerning my own private interest.

Hasted next refers to the forthcoming sale of his manuscripts and excuses himself from allowing Boys to purchase certain items which the latter had selected without taking the whole collection on the grounds that this would spoil the sale. Finally the historian tells Boteler of his intention to acknowledge his indebtedness to him in the preface to the fourth volume of the *History*.

At this stage of the correspondence there are altogether six letters from Hasted to Boteler without a single surviving letter the other way, although at least four are acknowledged in Hasted's letters. One of these acknowledgements, in a letter dated 6 February 1796, refers in typical modern business jargon to 'your last kind favor'. The early part of the letter is particularly concerned with the graphic aspects of the *History,* such as vignettes, plates and plans of entrenchments. Hasted then gives his reply to Boteler's offer to correct proofs of the parishes about which he was specially knowledgeable:

> Readily should I have embraced your kind offer of sending you the respective sheets before they were put to the press but that is truly out

of my power for Mr. Simmons has the whole MS. copy and as to the proof sheets, even that is likewise so from the day they are printed off and have had the printer's first correction, they are sent per post to me here for my correction and then returned the same night to them again, so that my distance from them makes the further delay impossible, otherwise you may be certain I should have accepted your kind offer of it with many thanks as highly *beneficial* and I may say *necessary* for the ultimate revision of my *History*.

It became apparent that Boteler himself was thinking of turning his hand to a history, most probably of his home village of Eastry, and was a bit worried whether by supplying material to Hasted he might be debarred from later using it for himself, but Hasted does his best to remove this anxiety with the assurance that 'You are I think in no danger of the aspersion of plundering from me; it is an apprehension that should by no means deter you from any design of the kind you mention, and if you go on with it, my best wishes are for your success and satisfaction in it'.

The great problem of giving a correct and accurate account of the exploits of the late Captain John Harvey is ventilated.[2] Hasted invites Boteler, who was a kinsman of Harvey, having married his sister, to write out the account of Harvey's heroism himself:

> I shall insert it with the greatest pleasure if you will indite and send it to me to place, as a note, after the mention of him in manner as you will frequently observe in my former volume and should I make any alteration you shall see it before it is printed for your approbation.

This letter is full of interest, and we next have a reference to the forthcoming sale of Hasted's manuscripts:

> My MSS. *altogether* will be sold by auction, with another large collection the latter end of this month, or the next, of which I will take care you shall have a catalogue in due time. I don't suppose so trifling a matter can bring you to Town, but should you have other occasion to come to Town you may take the opportunity of taking this sale at the same time. Whenever you do I hope for the favor of your calling on me that I may have the satisfaction of hearing *from yourself* your Pardon for the last unaccountable reception I gave you when I last saw you here after the trouble you had taken to come so far to me in such a place.

The great significance of this passage did not appear until much later in the investigation. It helped to correct a mistaken idea which had prevailed for more than a century.

A letter of 30 June 1796 acknowledges another 'favor' of Boteler (which has yet to be traced) 'which I had given up all hopes of, since the severe and unforgiving sentence passed on me by my long and constant friend and benefactor Mr. Boys of writing to me no more'. Hasted continues:

I dare say sir you have been long ere now made acquainted with it and the cause of it—a cause which tho' it may have existed, I may truly say I was in fact innocent of, for, from my present situation I was debarred months before of looking over the MSS. I was forced to trust to others to peruse and delete from them those which were unfit for the eyes of the public and I truly thought that I had myself in possession every letter of Mr. Boys either of a private nature or which could give any umbrage otherwise. Unhappy I am, unhappy indeed, that he thinks it not so, and that there were left, unknown to me, those which have deprived me of his most valuable esteem, and friendship, a loss which has affected me more than imprisonment or any other misfortune from my birth to the present moment. With sorrow of heart I deplore it at this very moment. Is there no mitigation, no forgiveness for an old friend who has unintentionally offended? I would not have offended him, as I call God to witness, for forty times the value; I would have perished; I would have starved before I would have done it. Let me, Sir, by every entreaty, by every appeal to your feelings implore you to intercede for me for his forgiveness, for him to obliterate from his memory this unhappy break of our friendship and to restore me to the same place in his esteem. I shall ever acknowledge your goodness in it; with gratitude I shall acknowledge it, in addition to the many instances I have received of your friendship to me. Do, my good Sir, try your influence with him and make me happy by letting me know you have succeeded for me.

But Hasted quickly switches from emotion to business and after some talk about a loan of plates of Eastry church he offers to let Boteler see the account of the Eastry Hundred *after* it has been printed, but not before, and says in effect that if Boteler does not hurry up and supply the account of Admiral (*sic*) Harvey he (Hasted) will have to rely on the *Gentleman's Magazine* for the details. Lastly we hear of the historian's ineffectual efforts to get released from the gaol:

Tho I have more than once entirely satisfied my plaintiff and obtained his good will for my release hence, yet a malicious attorney has ever stepped between, and rendered this agreement void so that unless providence interferes by his removal in some measure or other I fear my doom will be to languish here in misery and want and my only comfort remains in the kindness of those friends who have not forgot me in my adversity. You sir have been liberally good to me, so has Mr. Boys alas I must yet let him be ever so implacable, style him the best [of men] to me who I am not ashamed to own must have perished had it not been for his goodness.

The earlier part of Hasted's next letter, dated 9 July, is concerned with the wording to go on an engraving of Eastry church to be dedicated to Boteler, while the latter part returns to the theme of Boys' estrangement:

I fear you have had no success in obtaining me a return of Mr. Boys' friendship. If he persists in blotting out from his memory all former kind and feeling sensations of it which he for so many years taught me to believe he had for me and which I have in every instance so continually experienced from him; if I cannot obtain his pardon for an involuntary fault which I never intended to commit and was totally ignorant that I had offended in it, I must submit to his pleasure in it, but I cannot say but I think it rather a harsh and cruel resolution on so old a friend as myself and this in the time of my adversity. It shews as if he thought me ungrateful to him, which I would perish rather than be guilty of. But I beg your pardon sir for thus troubling you in an affair which relates unhappily to myself and here it must rest in future silence till it meets with forgiveness elsewhere.

Exactly a month later comes another letter from which we learn of Boys' reconciliation with Hasted:

I must first thank you for your additional act of goodness in regaining me the friendship of Mr. Boys, who has at last written to me a most kind and friendly letter, a balmy comfort to me in my distressful situation. This comfort indeed I have, and it is no small one, that in that fallen situation which in general carries the loss of every friend I have found hardly one who has not afforded me every assistance and attention, and among them none more essentially so than yourself and Mr. Boys.

After more about the inscription on the plate of Eastry church Hasted returns to the vexed question of the submission of proofs:

The account of my History of Eastry Parish is just printed. I wish time had been consistent with the Press to have submitted the proofs to you. It could not be and I was forced to acquiese but I have desired Mr. Simmons to send, in my name, to you a fair copy of these sheets and to beg your kind acceptance of them.

We have more about Captain Harvey, and then comes this passage:

I have but just now had an opportunity of the loan of Mr. Douglas's *Nenia Britain (Britannica)*; he is most pompous I see in his quotations, much more I think than is necessary for the subject of his work and seems as if meant to shew how many books he had turned over for the purpose. In his criterion of the ages and nation of the tumuli he describes, he affects to settle both by differing from others and at last leaving both in as much doubt in his own mind as when he undertook them at first. His Plates are very pretty and pleasingly done. I have copied some few, among which are Coldred church and fortification, St. Margaret's, the Sheperdswell and Chartham Barrows some of which I think I shall make use of if you tell me they are sufficiently accurate.

In his critism of Douglas, Hasted seems to be attacking one who was perhaps greater than himself and if an ample quotation of authorities is a sign of vanity, which it is not, who would be more guilty than Hasted himself? For a barefaced announcement of intended plagiarism this passage would take some beating; and we note than in prison Hasted seems to have had access to the latest books on the subjects that interested him.[3]

Fig. 5.   An archaeological drawing by James Douglas, from his *Nenia Britannica*.

The Roman Burial Ground at Ash near Sandwich.

Fig. 6.   Hasted's copy of Douglas's drawing. He treats it as a pretty view; all Douglas's explanatory lettering is omitted.

The letter is certainly one of the more important ones and contains an account in Hasted's own words of the genesis of the second edition of his *History*:

> I have within these few days executed an agreement with Mr. Bristow of Canterbury to print and publish an octavo edition of my *History,* in 8 volumes. It will be abridged of all tautologies and uninteresting matters; the subjects will be new arranged, the present state of parishes enlarged and to render it more pleasant and agreeable all the notes, excepting authorities, will be added in the text; the families and estates will be continued to the present time and the whole corrected and amended; the Parochial charities will be added complete throughout and the monuments and memorials in the western part of the County, omitted mostly in the first folio volume, will be added. The price of each volume including maps and vignettes 7s. 6d.; the folio prints of seats etc., about 9 in number to each volume may be had stitched in a Number in blue paper at about 6d. each print, to be had or not at the option of the purchaser of each volume; the first volume to be published in January and each succeeding volume in 5 months successively afterwards. His Advertisement of Proposals will come out next week. I hope you will approve of it. I have made a most safe and beneficial bargain with him, of profit to myself on the Publication.

Having delivered himself of this momentous news Hasted takes the opportunity of his better hopes for the future to shake Boteler down for a loan:

> . . . but till then I must feed alone on expectation. You sir have already been most liberal to me in my time of necessity. I dread to ask a further favor of you, but I am now, and shall be but for the assistance of my friends, in a state of unhappy necessity till the above time. Would you sir befriend me with a loan of 5 guineas. (I have not forgot your former liberal bounty, nor shall I ever forget it [until] January, the time of my 1st volume's publication, when I will sacredly repay you [out of] the first receipts from it. Indeed sir I am at in that crisis of want nothing less than which should drive me to request *so serious a mark of your friendship* to me. I will keep my promise punctually to you, with my continual acknowledgements for your goodness in it.

The letter ends with a progress report on the attempt to get the Lord Guilford to contribute a plate of his family seat at Waldershare. Nearly all these engravings were made at the expense of the nobility and gentry whose properties they publicised, and Hasted thus took advantage of their vanity to adorn his *History* with illustrations obtained free of cost.

There is a long gap before the next Boteler letter dated 3 September 1796. After another instalment of detail about the perennial topics of the entrenchments near Walmer and the engraving of Eastry church, Boteler, who obviously has received the printed-off sheets relating to Eastry, observes that, although the account is well drawn up and contains a great deal of matter, there are several inaccuracies, which he proceeds to enumerate. Hasted seems to have carried out his dire threat of taking the account of Captain Harvey's last fight from the *Gentleman's Magazine,* and, says Boteler:

The account of Captain Harvey's engagement is very erroneous. I know it was so described in the *Gentleman's Magazine* but as the family meant to draw up for the public an accurate account of the share he had in the action of the 1st of June it was not thought worth while to make any comments on it. Your reference however to the *Gentleman's Magazine* shews from whence you took it.

Some of the other criticisms relate to tiny matters of detail, the colouring of an item in someone's coat of arms and so forth, and some seem mere pinpricks, as when Hasted says that Eastry 'exhibits a picturesome appearance from every point of view', and Boteler, having presumably discovered one or more non-picturesque points of view, suggests that the word 'many' should be substituted for 'every'. But after this example of light sparring Boteler gets through Hasted's guard with a vengeance and delivers a knock-out blow to his solar plexus:

These are certainly errors not of the first magnitude, but could have been easily corrected had I been permitted to have seen the proof impression. You say that it was impossible, and that Mr. Simmons would not by any means consent to it from the delay it would occasion. It is with reluctance, I must confess, I mention a fact which I meant to have passed by but for your repeated declarations that it was your wish that it should have been submitted to the inspection of Mr. Boys and myself. Just as your 4th volume was going to the press we both offered to Mr. Simmons to overlook the proof impressions and assist in correcting any mistakes that might escape your notice: indeed we thought ourselves entitled to a privilege of this kind, lest from inadvertancy we might ourselves have contributed to propogate error, or that you might have mistaken our meaning. I wrote to you at the same time on the subject; and before I received your answer, happening to be at Canterbury, I called on Mr. Simmons, who assured me that he had in very pressing terms requested this permission from you, but that you had absolutely refused your consent. To justify himself he read a passage from your letter to him wherein you say that, after having conducted so far the whole of your work without assistance, you would not now submit it for correction to gratify the curiosity or indulge the vanity of anyone! Far indeed was any such motive from Mr. Boys or myself! We had but one object in view; to contribute what we could to make it perfect, and we thought from the misfortune of your situation the offer would have been gladly accepted as a convenience to you.
To return to the history of Eastry . . .

Boteler then demurs at what he considers to be the undue prominence that Hasted gives to Boteler's own family:

I could have wished that, under the article [. . .] Brook Street I and my family had not been brought quite so much in the foreground. I thank you for the kindness of your intentions, but fear that the public notice you have taken of my contributing to your work will make it surmised that it was drawn up by myself. Some parts might have been omitted, others shortened and yet the substance retained.

However, Boteler confesses himself *'upon the whole* much pleased' with Hasted's account.

There is more about Lord Guilford's engraving and the proposed checking of Douglas's illustrations, but before this comes a cryptic remark the high significance of which was not to become apparent for a long time. Boteler offers to check the maps of the Hundreds in East Kent and to 'contribute all in my power to render them more correct than they are at present: Andrews and Drury made a shocking work of their survey of this part of the county'.

Later in the same month, on 18 September, Boteler sends Hasted an engraving of Barfrestone church but explains that all further progress is put on one side because of the commencement of the shooting season, to which excuse Hasted replied that he did not for one moment wish to interfere with Boteler's diversions. In the event, however, the engraving was not immediately sent because, as Boteler explains in a short addendum dated a week later, he 'rolled it on a small stick intending to have sent it you last Sunday by the Post, but as the demand of Postage was more than I thought it ought to have been I declined sending it as I shall have an opportunity of doing it by means of a friend in the course of the ensuing week'.

This is an interesting sidelight on the 18th-century postal system. Hasted evidently received the parcel safely since by 4 November he has had the enclosure re-engraved and is returning it.

There is disappointing news of the progress of the printing of the fourth folio volume which 'thro the more weighty publications of Mr. S. (Simmons)—pocket books and almanacks, has stood still this month and more just on its entrance into Thanet so that I fear it will be a long time in its journey thro it'. More helpful is his account of the second (octavo) edition:

> The first volume of my octavo edition will be a very promising book.
> It is well printed both as to paper and letter (*sic*) and will be embellished
> with a number [of] pretty vignettes. I hope the reading will not be dis-
> approved of; the plates in the additional folio number being 8 will be
> improved and highly finished by one of the first engravers. What I feared
> most was compressing it within the promised bounds, which I am happy
> to find we can do.

Lastly Hasted appeals to Boteler to write more often and complains that Boys has ceased altogether to correspond.

After this there is a gap of more than a year in the correspondence, or at least in what we have of it. The next letter, one from Boteler dated 17 February 1798, refers to a letter of Hasted's of 29 January, which has disappeared. However, the topics do not seem to have changed much in the interim and we are back again with the plate of Eastry church, the problem now being the exact form of Boteler's arms which are to be displayed below it. Boteler had been twice married and he shows a sketch of his arms which include those of Harvey, Fuller and Paramor (families of his wives) in addition to his own.

Just as there are 'meaty' letters so there are some that are quite barren of interest. Hasted's letter of 30 March 1798 is of this kind. It deals with maps and plates and engravings. It acknowledges Boteler's 'last favor'; and in spite of the six weeks interval this is clearly the letter of 17 February.

In May Hasted was asking permission to send Boteler proofs of two maps for correction 'as early as possible, for we begin to wind up our long business to a short conclusion. When the work is completed I hope it will give satisfaction. I have done all my endeavours towards it and no small ones have they been'. He concludes:

> I hope whenever you may have an hour to throw away in town or country you will not forget an old friend in your sincere well wishes.

From Boteler's next letter a month later we find that the maps which Boteler (and Boys, as it now transpires) are to correct had reached Eastry in duplicate and one set had been sent to Boys who 'was most busily employed in fixing the position of all the churches in this corner of the county from General Roy's' observations: this will enable me to make a very correct map of these parts indeed'.

General Roy was a distinguished military engineer who made plans of Kent and other counties, using for the first time the accurate triangulation method on which the present ordnance survey is based.

In Boteler's next letter, dated 10 July, he acknowledges the receipt of the print of the engraving of Eastry church below which his arms are displayed. From his comments it is obvious that Hasted has had them printed exactly as recommended by Boteler in his earlier letter. Boteler seems to have forgotten what he had previously said and now contends that the arms so arranged signify 'that my first wife outlived my present'. Then Boteler sketches a layout which is the one which now appears beneath the engraving in the *History*. Boteler then reverts to a theme which runs more and more through the correspondence, the inaccuracy of Hasted's maps; they are 'so very incorrect that Mr. Boys and I are puzzled to know what to do with them. We will patch them up as well as we can, but I had much rather make them anew'.

And there is further disappointing news of the slow progress of Simmons, the printer, with the printing of the fourth folio volume.

The next letter, from Hasted, although dated two months later than the last seems to be an acknowledgement of it. The only interesting item in it is a direction by Hasted to 'send the parcel containing the corrected plans to Somerset Coffee House, Strand, if you have no other means of sending it to me'. This coffee house seems to have been a starting point of stage coaches and a kind of *poste restante* for correspondence. It is mentioned by Boswell.

Another month passes and Hasted has still not received his corrected maps and is becoming somewhat panic-stricken: 'I am in great want of them indeed, for I am called on, on every side for them with the most unpleasant importunities'. Yet he admits that he has recently been visited by Boys, with a companion, and completely forgot to mention the question of the maps: 'My thankfulness to him for the favor he did me in it' [i.e., in visiting the prison] 'absorbed every other thought whatever, and I neither had a thought of enquiring where the maps were, or when I might expect them'. There were, it seems, two maps, and Hasted suggests that the postage would be much less if each one was disguised as a single sheet letter. This to-ing and fro-ing with the maps continues for two letters more from which we learn at the end of October 1798 that the fourth folio volume is printed except for the index, etc., 'and the plates are all engraved and worked off excepting the maps. The last word about the maps seems to be the curious (wavy line) letter described earlier (page 13) with Boteler's despair of making them accurate and his do-it-yourself efforts to make them give a 'tolerable idea of the whole'.[4]

Hasted's letter of 14 March 1799 is significant as it covers the questionnaires about changes since 1792 which were discovered among the loose documents:

> I am become a petitioner to you again for your kind assistance and I hope it will be the last I shall have occasion to trouble you for. It is for (your kind assistance of) information relating to the changes and alterations which have happened since you sent me in 1792 an account of the places in your neighbourhood mentioned in the enclosed sheet. I hope I shall not put you to too much trouble in it as I trust by far the greatest part of them lye within your own knowledge. I shall be much obliged to you for them by the middle of next month, when I expect to be called on for them.

A feature of the first edition is its excellent indexing and this letter gives some idea of the hard work that it involved:

> The indexes to the folio volumes are now in the press and will continue printing without intermission till finished, so that there can be nothing now left to retard it. The indexes have been a horrid uphill labor to me and have cost me more than 4 months to compleat them. I assure you I had much rather write a whole folio volume than go thro the heavy drudgery of making them.

Boteler returned Hasted's questionnaires with very reasonable despatch (29 April 1799) leaving a few answers still outstanding which he promised to send in a few days. He had obtained the information about the Isle of Thanet from a local inhabitant, Mr. Garnett, and has enlisted the help of Bristow, the printer of the second edition, to get the packet to Hasted. Boteler's family modesty, whether real or simulated, again appears:

> Under the parish of Shepherdswell my sister will be obliged to you to omit in your octavo edition the encomium you have passed on the grounds round Upton Court (her residence). I apprehend that you do not descend to such minutiae, but at her request I have guarded you against it.

We hear the thunder of an approaching storm when Boteler remarks that he will send a few corrections for Eastry. His corrections must have been to the first edition and as the text had already been printed they must have been intended for inclusion in the Addenda and Corrigenda. However, we have no extant letter to prove directly that Boteler carried out his threat or promise, and, in fact, the relations between the two seem to have been unusually amicable at this time since the next letter is one from Hasted on 5 October in the same year, in which he asks whether Boteler will, as a great favour, consent to have the eighth octavo volume (second edition) dedicated to him. In the meantime the fourth volume of the first edition has at last been published and Hasted assumes that Boteler has got his copy:

> I dread your acute remarks and criticisms on it but in excuse for the many errors in it let my distance from the press and every other embarrassment I labored under during the whole time of its being in the press plead my excuse. I am myself truly conscious of the demerits of the volume, and as such, submit to every censure the author of it deserves for his faults throughout it.

He then refers to the recent great fire at the King's Bench prison:

> By the help of good friends I am tolerably well recovered from my losses by the dreadful fire here, and indeed with much greater comfort than I was before and when I begin to taste the fruits of my fourth volume I shall be made still more so.

Less pleasant is the receipt of Simmons' bill for the printing which is, Hasted exclaims, 'beyond all belief. No less a sum than £1,100 all of which he must be paid before I can receive a shilling from it'.

Peace still reigns when Boteler next writes at the end of the same month when his concern is with the vignette to accompany the dedication of volume eight of the second edition. There is a slight difference of opinion about the artist's having depicted aquatic plants in a foreground which, in fact, consists of a dry meadow. There is also much discussion of the supply of plates and engravings by Hasted to Boteler which only makes sense if, as we must now consider as established, the first edition was published unbound. Boteler supplies a list of the plates which he has already received and asked Hasted to let him have the balance. This obviously presupposes that these illustrations are loose, and not bound into the books.

Boteler's next two letters are long and important and, although their general purport is obvious, the vast amount of detail that they contain raises many difficulties. The first letter, of 25 February 1800, covers a long list of errors discovered by Boteler in the ninth octavo volume, and the second, dated 2 March, has a similar list of corrections for the 10th volume; with the vital difference that when it came to volume 10, which included Boteler's own native heath of Eastry, he was not content merely to put forward a list of suggested amendments but went further and, getting hold of the printer's proofs, induced the printer to let him make alterations in some of them before sending them to Hasted.

The first letter runs as follows:

> The foregoing observations on your ninth volume are such as I have thought proper to send you, some of which you undoubtedly will think worth notice. I have received from Mr. Bristow the foul proofs of the tenth volume as far as are printed off and I am running them over. I am much concerned that I did not see a proof sheet of the parish of Eastry,

> as I think I should have prevailed on you to omit a great part of the
> mention you have made of my family. I do not see that you have, in
> your abridged edition, taken as much notice of any other; and as you
> have been pleased to acknowledge my little assistance so publicly, it will
> appear to many that I have sought by it an indulgence to my vanity. If
> you will allow me to cancel an ½ sheet of it, I can remove a great part
> of that which hurts my feelings. I have consulted Bristow upon it who,
> with your consent, is willing that it should be done; and you will of
> course suppose that I mean to be at the expense of it. With your appro-
> bation I would send you the ½ sheet in question with my proposed
> alterations; and as I should in no respect interfere with the matter, but
> only amplify your subjects with an equal number of words to allow for
> the continuance in the next page, I hope it will not offend *your* feelings
> by my thus interfering. You will be so good as to let me know your
> determination on this head, as whatever is done I find must be done out
> of hand.

Boys, we hear, may have become incapable of assisting further:

> Alas! he is far removed from his former self. Two successive fits, border-
> ing on paralytic strokes, have given such a shock to his mortal powers, and
> so much impaired his memory, that I doubt of his ability to assist you
> on this occasion. I will however introduce the subject to him as he now
> seems to be much recovered, and I shall soon be able to discern whether
> he be competent to the task.

A feature of the list of alterations to the ninth volume is that in two instances
Boteler says that the mistake has already been drawn to Hasted's attention by
letter, the one presumably that Boteler had promised to send in his communication
of 29 April.

It seems that Hasted sent a reply justifying to some extent the amount of space
devoted to the Boteler family but we only know about this letter from Boteler's
reference to it the next time he wrote, on 2 March, carrying out his promise to
alter the famous half-sheet of volume 10:

> On the other side you see my proposed alteration in an half sheet of
> your work. I was aware that I must not lose sight of the folio edition
> in any change of the matter, and your letter has had the effect upon me
> of retaining much more relative to my family than I at first proposed. You
> will see many of my alterations are corrections of errors, and of some
> points relative to my ancestry which cannot be substantiated . . . Where
> everything asserted can be proved I have no great objection to the retain-
> ing it, and I would not wish to conceal that I have some satisfaction in
> knowing who my ancestors were; your observations on this point I
> perfectly coincide with but I would not wish to parade too much the
> occasion, nor that my own name should be too often brought forward
> [. . .] the expressions in your dedication have contributed to [make me]
> shy on this head.

Boteler was evidently contemplating further corrections and suggestions but
uncertain whether he could get them to Hasted in time to be printed. 'Do you

conclude your *History* with the tenth volume and would you not wish to have [my] observations to add to the end of it? If so, how long will it be before you publish? I can soon finish the task; indeed I have already run through great part of it'. This is a clear reference to Hasted's frequent practice of inserting at the end of a volume addenda and corrigenda of the *previous* volume. Obviously if volume 10 was to be the last one there would be no volume 11 to carry Boteler's amendments and they must therefore be made quickly enough to be printed with volume 10 itself. As regards the 'Eastry half-sheet' Boteler was intending to have his amendments (which included a rewrite of the whole of page 99) inserted into the text itself, this being the primary object of the present letter.

A few days later (1 May) Boteler sends a letter on two folds of which are written his suggested amendments to the 10th volume (outside the Eastry half-sheet). On the third page Boteler promises a view of Deal Castle and commends to Hasted the alterations to the half-sheet (sent earlier) but says nothing of the amendments that are inscribed on the first two pages. Hasted swallowed his pride, accepted the amended half-sheet virtually as it stood and included the extra amendments in the 'Additions, etc.' at the end of the volume. Bristow the printer had popped a £1 bank note into Boteler's letter, with a brief explanation. He had his own opinion, it would seem, as to what kind of oil was most likely to calm the troubled waters.

This is the end of the correspondence about the composition, printing and illustrating of the *History*. In the interim, on 24 March 1800, Hasted had written the last extant letter from the gaol; it had nothing to do with the amendments of volumes 9 and 10. Boteler wanted information about Eastry from the British Museum, and was intending to solicit the help of Thomas Astle. Hasted offered a letter of introduction, with a few hints to Boteler as to how to find his way round his (Hasted's) manuscripts in the museum, and also offered him the chance to peruse the two commonplace books (now part of the Irby deposit) in his possession:

> Dear Sir,
> However thankful I may be for every instance of your kind friendship I am truly ashamed of being a constant beggar to you, and that the pleasure I receive in your visits should be subject to a constant Sunday's Toll. I think now you can have no further excuse for my being a further burden to you, but that I shall have the pleasure of seeing you (and a pleasure it always will be to me) gratis. A thousand thanks to you for every favor I have so kindly received from you.
> You wish much to have an opportunity of speaking to Mr. Astle. He and I have been upon a brotherly footing of friendship for these 30 years and upwards. Will you accept a letter from me telling him so, which you may carry to him Wednesday or Thursday at your pleasure. He will I know receive you with much friendly behaviour, not only on my account but on your own too and it will save you, at least, that awkward business of telling who you are, yourself. He is to be met with generally at the Paper Office, Scotland Yard, between one and two on any day and if you will let me know this afternoon by Penny Post I will return you the letter by tomorrow morning, as you may choose to go to-morrow.

When you go to the British Museum remember that they have among my MSS. the 2 quarto volumes of Index to them which have the several parishes & Eastry among them alphabetically arranged. Perhaps you may meet with something you may like to look at among them. I have likewise here 2 folio volumes arranged in like manner which refers [sic] to all the printed books, I believe all of them in print which have been published. Eastry is among them of course. Should you like to peruse these here, it may serve you a multiplicity of reading and may perhaps give you some information which you are not already possessed of.

I have some other matters which I wish to write to you on but the Post going out will not permit me. Expecting the favor of your answer I remain, Dr. sir, your obliged and faithfull servant

King's College   Edward Hasted
Southwark
    March 24th, 1800

This letter is significant for the sidelights it throws on Hasted's circumstances. When he speaks of a constant 'Sunday's Toll' one imagines this to mean that every time Boteler paid a visit he had in effect to put his coin in the collection box.

The two remaining letters that we have were written after an interval of some three years, by which time Hasted has at last been released from the prison and is living at No. 5 Greenhouse Row, Westminster Road, Surry (sic). Boteler forwards an enquiry about the ancestors of Mr. Henry Boys, obviously a connection of our old acquaintance William who is now (alas!) described by Boteler as 'our late friend'. Evidently Hasted's circumstances were regarded as still being reduced because Boteler sends a guinea note to repay the little expenses attending the enquiry. The last letter of all is dated 24 November in the same year and in it Hasted acknowledges another letter from Boteler which we do not have. Without Boteler's letter Hasted's reply is not very comprehensible, the subject matter being a certain volume of the second edition which somebody was trying to obtain for somebody else.

What does this correspondence tell us? Most of the letters speak for themselves and the general impression is of Boteler anxious to do all he can to help but somewhat frustrated by Hasted's jealous vanity and obstinate reluctance to admit of any correction prior to the printing of his text. After that he is prepared to accept any emendation and insert it without question in his addenda and corrigenda. On the other hand, the correspondence shows up Hasted's great energy and zeal, particularly in preparing, obviously at the cost of great personal travail, the excellent indexes which so distinguish his *History*. We also note that he was most conscientious in bringing all the facts up to date, the last questionnaire being completed in the spring of the very year when publication was to take place.

This seems as good a place as any to mention the solution of the problem of Hasted's maps. When they came to describe these the weavers of the Hasted legend excelled themselves somewhat; not content with generalised praise on the lines of the gentleman from the *Leather Bottle* at Southfleet[5] they became quite specific.

The *History* contains a small-scale map of the county and is interspersed with maps on the scale of two inches to a mile for each Hundred, or sometimes for two Hundreds. It was supposed that for the purpose of making these maps a new survey of the county and all its 66 Hundreds was undertaken 'at truly daunting expense'. The result 'was an immense improvement on anything that had gone before—indeed in most cases there was nothing earlier'. It was thought that Hasted often accompanied the surveyors in their work in the field. Note the two assertions: first, a survey was made specially for Hasted's maps; second, that there had been in many cases 'nothing earlier'. What do Hasted's correspondents tell us about all this?

First, and most surprisingly, in view of the survey, that the maps were terribly inaccurate. Boteler's despair of making anything satisfactory out of the east Kent maps[6] is almost exactly echoed in faraway Bredhurst, where Mr. Cromp found the map of his district 'so amazingly incorrect that I scarce see how it can be rectified'. John Thorpe tells Hasted of his efforts to correct for Bayly, the engraver, 'many omissions and mistakes that have come within the compass of my knowledge'.[7] Then there are casual remarks which imply that no survey had been made. A correspondent says of the Hundred of Eyhorne that 'a survey would be necessary to ascertain the boundaries which, I apprehend, you think too expensive'. At Wrotham, Mr. Hodges somewhat similarly observed that he has made the best amendment in his power without a survey; he has corrected 'the most flagrant errors' but the map is still incorrect in many places. The amateurish methods for attempting to secure some semblance of accuracy tell their own tale. Thorpe lent Bayly a copy of Kilburne's *Survey of Kent* 'which he says is of great service to him'. The engraver was responsible for more than reproducing a design handed to him—he was expected to make good its deficiencies with the aid of Kilburne's book and Thorpe's hints.

Amongst Hasted's papers was the draft of the map of the Lowy (environs) of Tonbridge. Two sections of an earlier map are pinned one to the other and bear freehand alterations of the most slovenly character put in by Hasted, including a generous diaper throughout of symbols indicating trees. The maps are very inaccurate, not only according to contemporary critics but from modern observation. Buildings are placed in completely wrong situations, a broad river, of which no modern trace can be seen, flows up hill and down dale, and in at least one case a village is shown miles away from its real situation.

Legend murmurs defensively that Hasted did not have the advantage that a modern writer would have of the Ordnance Survey which came 'a generation later'. This excuse may stand good for the earlier volumes but certainly not for the fourth folio volume. Colonel William Mudge's Ordnance Map of Kent based on a trigonometrical survey admittedly appeared two years (a very short 'generation') after the publication of the fourth folio volume,[8] but large parts of Kent had been mapped (accurately one assumes) by Colonel Mudge's predecessor, General Roy, half a century before, and from 1791 the official ordnance survey (or trigonometrical survey as it was termed) was in progress. What exactly would have been available to Hasted had he wished to take advantage of these more modern productions we do not know exactly, but he certainly knew of them since General Roy had described his methods in the *Philosophical Transactions* of the Royal Society of which Hasted was a Fellow. In fact, the historian took from Roy's findings the distance between

Dover Castle and Calais Cathedral. William Boys, too, had used Roy's 'triangles' to plot the position of the churches in east Kent, an exercise which showed up the badness of Hasted's maps.

How, then, did Hasted prepare them, and what was the material deposited on Bayly's drawing board with perhaps some instructions concerning revisions and alterations? This seemed an insoluble mystery until, after it had been discovered how much Hasted relied on the books of the Canterbury Cathedral library for his research, a look was taken at the maps and atlases in the repository which would have been there in Hasted's time. As soon as Andrews and Drury's *Atlas of Kent* (1769) was opened the mystery was solved; take any of Hasted's maps and compare them with the corresponding section of the Andrews and Drury atlas and their source is at once apparent. Apparent, too, is the relevance of Boteler's observation that Andrews and Drury 'made a shocking work' of their survey of east Kent.[9] A piece of the Drury atlas was found amongst Hasted's papers.

It is time, surely, to look once again at the historian's statement which seems to claim originality for his maps. The relevant words are: 'The maps of the several hundreds . . . are the first which have been attempted of the kind for this county'. He must be taken to mean that this is the first time that anybody has tried to show the *boundaries of the Hundreds* in Kent. In this respect, and in this respect alone, his maps may well be original.

Chapter Five

AN ARMY OF HELPERS

MY SELF-IMPOSED TASK had, at the beginning, taken the form of a weekly visit to the cathedral library to do a stint of a few hours conscientious and hopefully useful, work on the records—no more than was necessary to satisfy a pensioner's conscience. At the end it involved an almost continuous round of activity, using not only Hasted's manuscripts but also a vast accumulation of files of correspondence, notes, and photocopies of documents, gleaned from half-a-dozen different repositories and from scores of different books, not to mention a small library of indispensable printed volumes, ancient and modern.

The watershed between the two phases was reached with the cataloguing of Hasted's correspondence portfolios. The voluminous material consisted basically of letters addressed to him but there were, here and there, pages of notes on pedigrees and so forth, in various hands. The items in the first portfolio had been marked by Hasted numerically: Volume 1 beings nos 1-132, and Volume 2 1-205, while the second portfolio of about the same size had 321 items, all relating to F III. Each item was endorsed in pencil in Hasted's hand with the name or names of the places concerned, and the items were filed in the order in which the places appeared in the *History*. In most cases the writers of the letters could be identified because they were mentioned in its text.

After some weeks of slow progress it became apparent that at my present pace the task might never be completed. Moreover, the whole picture had been changed by the discovery of the importance and significance of the Irby matter in general; the task had also become much more attractive when the far-from-promising mass of dry-looking manuscripts had revealed iself as a store of interesting facts and as a medium of introduction to interesting people who were already, from their signatures, handwriting and self-revealing traits, becoming familiar acquaintances. Boteler was fussy but informative; Boys, calm, stolid and full of facts; Deedes, urbane and helpful while busily engaged in building his family's fortunes: Brydges, also helpful, but patronising and vain over his possessions; and Lyon, garulous, enthusiastic and apparently omniscient; and, lastly, the central figure of Hasted himself was emerging as fallible and rather dull and stodgy, given now and then to prevarication bordering on deceitfulness, but atoning for his faults by his dedication to his task, boundless energy, and obstinate courage in the deepest adversity.

The mere calendaring of documents had indeed turned into an enlarged and quite different enquiry, but what effort would be needed to complete the work within a reasonable time, and would the result justify such an effort? Three months' hard work would suffice, Miss Oakley predicted, to get rid of the correspondence portfolios; and the operation would certainly be worthwhile since Hasted was an important figure. Much more time must therefore be devoted in future to the project; the *dilettante* approach must be abandoned and the investigation tackled as a serious job of work. At the same time, methods and intellectual tools must be overhauled.

Since the *second* edition was now revealed as a mere abridgement, the basis of my research must henceforth be the *first,* and if necessary work already done must be revised. I already had my own mutilated copy of the folio. I now obtained also a copy of Philipott's *Villare Cantianum* on indefinite loan from a friend, and invested in a micro-copy of the *Dictionary of National Biography*. A humble but necessary asset was a comprehensive list of all the six hundred-odd parishes and places in Kent, noting which volumes of F and O dealt with them. Hasted's texts were indexed only volume by volume, and in the course of preparing the list I soon found that his lists of parishes in F were incomplete.

I read all of Hasted's Prefaces, the long one preceding F I, the shorter ones for the succeeding volumes, and the garbled selection from all of them (with additions) that was printed for the second edition.

The cataloguing, listing the dates of the letters, names and status of the writers, subject matter and use made of it in the *History* took more than the expected three months, but the resulting tabulated information was of inestimable value for the future researches.

Among the more exotic items in the portfolios were two sections cut from an engraved map, pinned together and heavily altered freehand in ink, which were evidently the engraver's copy for the map of the Lowy of Tonbridge mentioned earlier; four pages of printer's proof of the account of Ash, near Sandwich; and a series of tracings on very thin paper evidently made by the engraver Godfrey as a preliminary to his drawings of the tombs and monuments in Chevening church. Almost without exception the letters are replies to queries by Hasted, and the variety of the information that he must have requested is quite astonishing. Most of it concerns the landowning families and their estates, pedigrees and armorial bearings. Which of the properties are manors? How far does the jurisdiction of the manor extend? Medieval incidents of tenure, fee-farm rents and royal franchises are other objects of the historian's curiosity. The feats of the gentry's ancestors, the law cases in which they had been involved, and the tombs in which they are buried are also of interest. Of equal importance but less in number are the enquiries about matters ecclesiastical—tithes, glebe, lists of rectors, vicars and curates, church monuments and church bells, patronage and pensions, not to mention the parochial charities and endowed schools. We are reminded that the *History* is also a topographical survey, so that, not satisfied with descriptions of the parishes and their soils, Hasted is interested in specially large trees, rivers, springs (especially if possessing legendary or actual healing or medicinal powers), swamps and marshes; the names and areas of the principal farms, public buildings, lighthouses, barracks and bridges; not forgetting the records or memories of noteworthy calamities—fires, storms and collapses of important buildings; old customs and legends; archaeological features and finds, megalithic monuments, ancient camps and Roman remains. Hasted wished also to have the administrative picture: the powers, charters and customs of the municipal corporations, the boundaries of the hundreds, the frequency of the holding of the manorial courts and their status as courts baron or more importantly as courts leet. Local finance and poor relief and the numbers of the population also engaged his attention. Studying the calendar one can see that the letters represent an information-gathering process which went through various stages. Noteworthy are some 28 questionnaires affecting as a rule several parishes, each with a number of manors or places within them. The questions are in Hasted's hand and are usually headed 'Manors and Places of Note'. Most of these questionnaires refer to the last owners of the properties recorded by Philipott in his *Villare Cantianum* (1659) and enquire about subsequent developments, including the then current ownerships.

The earliest letters date from the 1760s; the latest were received in 1789 just before the publication of volume III. The bulk, dated in the 1770s and 1780s, seem to have been sent as follow-ups of Hasted's perambulations, and by noticing the dates one can see when he was busy writing up the respective parishes. Some of the earlier letters were written up to 30 years before the accounts of the places were to appear in the *History,* and seem to be relics of a plan of writing which was later modified or abandoned.

Briefly, the correspondents who supplied these varied facts represent the aristocracy and landed gentry of Kent, with the Law and the Church also very prominent; some fifty of these contributors are persons of sufficient distinction to be the subject of articles in the *Dictionary of National Biography* and there are many interesting and amusing characters among them.

In his Preface Hasted acknowledges his special debt to the men of the Law and many of his informants' letters are impressed with the hallmarks of precision and accuracy that reveal the attorney, even where there is no other indication of the writer's profession. At a later stage an alphabetical list of all the informants was compared with the Law Lists of the period which the Law Society keeps in its library; no less than 29 of the correspondents turned out to have been attorneys. Some of the most important informants we have already met in these pages; others will appear later as the Hasted story develops. Some forty persons of distinction who answered Hasted's queries, most of whom are not otherwise mentioned in the narrative, have brief biographies later in this chapter.

The letters, as a collection, are of obvious interest to students of Hasted's work, illustrating his methods and showing the source of innumerable passages of his text. The perusal of their texts would have little attraction for the general reader, while the specialist may refer to the calendars lodged in the cathedral library at Canterbury and to the letters themselves. At the same time there are a fair number of letters that seem worth reproducing here for one reason or another— the eminence of the writer, some unusually fascinating tit-bit of information or graphic illustration of the relations between writer and recipient.

The letter of Thomas Austen which heads the selection is included merely as the outpourings of an eccentric, but the next letter comes from one who was probably the greatest man amongst Hasted's informants, Sir Joseph Banks, botanist and associate of Captain Cook, who relates his own exploits in the Pacific and in Iceland. The third correspondent selected is Thomas Astle with whom we are already acquainted. His letters, as it now transpires, form part of a correspondence to which Hasted's contributions were published 70 years ago. The newly-discovered material has some interesting references to John Wilkes.

The correspondence files produce a new character in the Hasted story worthy almost to stand beside William Boteler himself as a coadjutor; he is John Thorpe the younger, a celebrated Kentish antiquarian, from whom at least as many letters are preserved as from the energetic physician of Eastry. After the extracts from Thorpe's letters we have three items with a primatial flavour, one communication from the son of Archbishop Potter and two from Archbishop Secker himself. Kept until last is the correspondence between Lord Dacre and the historian; though quite prosaic on the surface it in fact raised some puzzling doubts which when thoroughly investigated produced the first of the series of unexpected discoveries that were to result from my investigation.

Austen, Thomas (d. 1790)

Vicar of Allhallows (Hoo) Austen had been a Minor Canon of Rochester Cathedral. Hasted describes him as 'a curious searcher into the antiquities of this county and a communicative worthy gentleman'. The following is the latter part of the long letter that he addressed to the historian:

December 2nd, 1778

As to Wouldham; my nervous system is so weak and tender at prest. that I can't walk above 2 mile & half & back again; and use a horse I cannot at any rate; so that you must depend only on what our friend Tresse can do for us, as he help'd Mr. Thorpe to sketches and Descriptions at Gillingham & Lidging Chapel. & I know half a word to him will influence him. The curate of Wouldham & Burham lives near me. I know the curates of Cuxton, Halling, Shorne, Cobham & ye next parish to it, the vicar of Frinsbury, &c., &c., whom I could employ to ask questions of farmers seen at Church, but if Double Duty be ye case, they may not have time to go to their houses, tho' I could write a note, to be answd. ye next Sundays, &c. I would readily promote yr. glorious work (such high Honor to our County) if I could; and this partly from a motive call'd *the pleasures of Imagination* in a retrospect of times past: for you must know that I was born on Chatham brook, next door but one to your good Grandfather & Grandmother on father's side who were extremely intimate with my mother &c. I reverence their memory (the poor old lady latterly fell down & broke her arm one Sunday morn. going to Church & seldom went out after. On Whits. Mond. June 3rd 1723 she stood godmothr. to my brothr. ye next eldest to me, & such connections then were valuable events: oh, the fine grapes, pears, &c. we boys enjoy'd. from her garden near the market place!) (I could tell you more of wht. I remembr., perfectly, when in Linen frocks & not older than 4 or 5 years.)

Topographical Anecdotes

The late 'Squire Chevins I suppose of Northfleet, as the newspapers related July 1st, 1768, or another Gentn. there, had in his Garden then ye very same identical female *Tortoise* wch. was first brought into Engld.

by Mr. Dampier, ye famous s. sea voyager; thereby proving the vast longevity of that Creature.

Austen then retails some instances, going back to 1733 of the discovery of Roman coins and pots in the district, and resumes:

Catesby's 4to. catalogue of MSS. in the Cotton Library belonging to Rochester and Canterbury Priories gives a curious account of how often ye books (by memorandums wrote in them) were pawn'd & redeem'd, for how-much; upon what condition given to such & such persons; odd physical Receipts, for the *Faevoir Pestelaunt* &c., &c.; very odd particulars worth notice for a Kentish Historian. I made abstracts of all these (at your *command* any day). I lately hinted to Mr. Thorpe for you, ye engraving in Dr. Rawlingson's *English Topographer,* large 8vo., of a *Cliff* seal (tho' you have Dispatch'd that Parish) found on *Blackheath,* wch. I wou'd tear out of the book for you, if need be; Mr. Tresse now has ye book, & I desired him to Draw a sketch of it for you; it might do in your *Addenda* perhaps, as it is very plain, & small one. I told him, Mr. Thorpe, of a few more anecdotes found in Lady Russel's Letters, & some State Papers; particrly. what *Cole's memoirs of State,* in folio say thus: 'AD.1697. It had been represented to the King by *Thomas Rider, Esq.* (of Boughton, I suppose) of Kent, that his father *Sir Willm. Rider,* during his abode at Venice, did Lend 20,000 Ducats to the Bank there several years ago, some part whereof had since been paid; but there yet remained a considerable arrear standing postponed in the books of ye said Bank: on 21 Sept. 1697 Charles, Earl of Manchester, Ambassador at Venice, was directed to interpose in his Majesty's name with the said State in order to procure that Justice be done to the said *Rider,* by discharging the said Debt, which had been so long delayed upon groundless pretences'. So far *Cole.* AD. 1686, July. Sir Willm. Coventry died at *Tunbridge,* & was buried at *Penthurst* in Kent. He left a noble charity, of 2000£ to the French Refugees lately come to Canterb. &c. (& 3000£ to redeem slaves), (Lady Russel's Letters.)
    I sometimes can recollect a thousand particulars either read of or told me, relative to our parishes in Kent, but at present may only seem to be impertinent, & detain you from more important concerns. Your work astonishes me at ye sight of your infine numbr. of authentic vouchers, the regular Detail of Pedigrees, accuracy of dates, variety of Interesting and Entertaining matter, expressiveness & compact run of the style, without ye least Tautology, the elegant & regular form of your method, throughout, & most ample Indexes, &c. and I hereby *acknowledge my most Grateful Thanks to you* that tho' my scanty fortune won't let me purchase large books, after spending so much already that way, & hence could not subscribe yet you was pleased to take *such generous notice* of a poor obscure vicar of Alhallows, in Hoo. This I discovered by the Loan of your Book to me from my most ingenious friend Mr. Tresse, but after a very little transient Peep at it, I told him there was in it such a large work for a studious & contemplative man, that I soon returned it (being then busy in copying a large work I have in hand, of a Diary of my own Life, Kept of all remarkable occurrences, regular, from August 1765 to this moment,

mixt. with a thousand anecdotes moral & entertaining; 40 vols. in 4to. each near 100 pages, I have wrote fair, & perhaps not one half ye work contains an innumerable many *surprizing* things, because *supernatural* ones) & told him I would borrow it again when disposed *to study very hard* our *Kentish* antiquities, as yours contain everything a man of curiosity need, or could wish, to know. I am vastly sorry to see the Clergy universally, are no better Benefactors to you. But *glory, & a true Patriot Spirit,* is your present motto. I am, most Ingenious & worthy Sir, Your sincere Friend, Tho: Austen.

Banks, Sir Joseph (1743-1820)

Sailed with Captain Cook as botanist on the voyage of the *Endeavour* to the Pacific (1769-71) and later became president of the Royal Society, which he ruled with a rod of iron. Though a patron of science rather than a worker, he nevertheless braved every danger on the voyage with Captain Cook in pursuit of botanical knowledge. He married a Hugessen heiress to inherit the picturesque seat of Provender, near Faversham, where Prince and Princess Romanoff lived until recently. Banks' letter, at Hasted's request, is about his own adventures:

> Soho Square,
> Feb. 26, 1782

Sir,

For your favor received by this night's post I am to return you my thanks. Your intention of making memorable mention of me in a work of such extensive utility as your *History of Kent* deserves that and more from me. To answer your questions however on that subject which you cannot be supposed acquainted with I shall be under the necessity of applying to the Heralds Office where everything that I know of relative to my family is lodged, as I would by all means wish to have your *History* agree in all particulars with the authentick records lodged there. I shall therefore immediately do it and forward to you the result of my application as soon as I can get it into my possession.

For what relates to myself personally I must beg leave to decline giving any opinion. I may flatter myself that being the first man of scientific education who undertook a voyage of discovery and that voyage of discovery being the first which turned out satisfactory to this enlightened age; that I was in some measure the first who gave that turn to such voyages or rather to their commander, Capt. Cook as guided and directed those which came after, as well as that in which I was personally concerned; but of this I must leave others to judge.

For myself otherwise I was born in London in the year 1743 Feb. 12/13 educated at Eton school and Christ Church Oxford, from whence I made my first voyage in the year 1765 to Newfoundland and Lisbon, returning in the spring 1766 with my friend Sir Thos. Adams, since decd. in His Majesty's Frigate *Niger*. After that in June 1767 I embarked on the voyage of discovery which was fitted out for the purpose of observing a transit of Venus. The account of this voyage being printed, I refer you to the book for information. On my return I was called upon to make a second voyage in a manner so flattering to myself that I did not hesitate. I provided a considerable establishment with the celebrated painter Zoffani as my draughtsman but the ship not answering the conveniences intended for me and my people I was under the necessity of either giving up the voyage or some of my people with most of the conveniences which were to enable them to answer many purposes of science which alone tempted me again to attempt the unknown ocean. Better than do my work by halves, the second time I determined to decline the whole, dissatisfied as I was with having scarce done only half my intended business, a sacrifice which I had then willingly made to my situation in life unknown to any one of my first outset. Disappointed as I was I employed some of my draughtsmen and others in a short voyage to Iceland in the year 1772 where I was fortunate enough to find the Island of Staffa which Mr. Pennant, who made at the same time a tour of the Western Islands for the sole purpose of visiting them, missed. For the account of it I refer you to his tour where he printed the words of my field journal, incorrect as they were, which I had lent him as a testimony that chance alone and not any intention of interfering with his pursuits had led me into his track.

My short stay in Iceland developed the singular wonder of Geiser and the summit of Heckla which had seldom if ever been visited by the natives; for the account of these I refer you to Troille's [Ummo von Troil] letters. He was a young Swede who being here upon his travels in England chose to accompany me in this tour and who since his departure home has been made Bishop of Lincimen [Linköpping] in Sweden.

Botany has been my favorite science since my childhood and the reason I have not published the account of my travels is that the first from want of time necessarily brought on by the many preparations to be made for my second voyage was entrusted to the care of Mr. Hawkesworth, and since that I have been engaged in a botanical work which I hope soon to publish as I have now near 700 folio plates prepared. It is to give an account of all the new plants discovered in my voyage round the world, somewhat above 800.

From my return from Iceland I lived in no particular station till Nov. 30 1779 when on the resignation of Sir John Pringle I was elected President of the Royal Society in which post I still remain.

If any further information is wanted by you I shall have great pleasure in communicating it and shall send you without delay the documents which I procure from the Heralds Office.

I am sir with gratitude for the intention which you have conceived of mentioning in your valuable book

Your faithful servant
JOS. BANKS

Astle, Thomas (1735-1803)

Perhaps Hasted's principal mentor. Astle held at one time or another some of the most important posts connected with the care of the public records of the kingdom, and his advice was constantly sought by the government of the day on such matters; he became Keeper of the Records in the Tower of London and a trustee of the British Museum, and wrote an important book on the subject of palaeography.

1. St John's Jerusalem, a gentleman's seat adapted from the remains of the Commandery of the Knights of St John. Hasted lived here 1757-70, and here conceived his plan to write the *History of Kent*.

2. A portrait of Edward Hasted from the British Library.

3. Edward Hasted, aged 45. From a portrait in the Maidstone Museum.

4. A portrait of Hasted in later life.

Edward Hasted at 69 1801 F.R.S. A.S.S.
Kentish Historian.
Depty Lieut. &c
the best & strongest likeness.

5. (below) The Cathedral Library, Canterbury, where many of Hasted's working papers for his *History* are deposited.

6. (*above*) The Hungerford Almshouses, Corsham, Wilts., where Hasted ended his days as master.

7. (*left*) Corsham Church, Wilts. Hasted was buried in the churchyard, but his grave is unmarked.

8. (*opposite, above*) Brook House, Eastry, Kent, home of William Boteler (1745-1818), Hasted's loyal friend and helper.

9. (*opposite, bottom left*) A curiously-shaped letter of William Boteler (see p. 13).

10. (*opposite, bottom right*) The riddle of Boteler's strange-looking letter explained.

Minster church in Thanet and the ruiny of the Abbey.

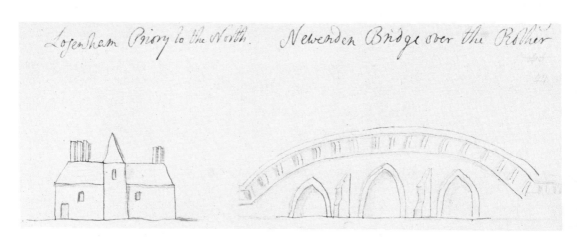

Lozenham Priory to the North.   Newenden Bridge over the Rother

Newenden to the South

11, 12, 13 & 14. A selection of the drawings copied by Hasted from Warburton's survey of Kent (1725), now included in Add. MS 5480 in the British Library.

Ostenghanger.

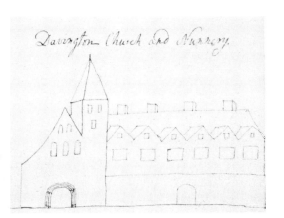

Davington Church and Nunnery.

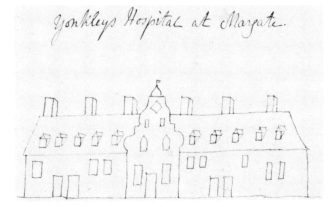

Yonkleys Hospital at Margate.

South Prospect of Hith

15, 16, 17 & 18. Drawings copied by Hasted from Warburton's survey of Kent.

Allington Castle

Midway River

Ruins of Beyham Priory

Eltham

19, 20 & 21.   Drawings copied by Hasted from Warburton's survey of Kent.

On 4 November 1763, Hasted wrote to Astle the first of the letters that were to be printed in *Archaeologia Cantiana*. He gives a long account of excavations made by Bryan Faussett, in Hasted's company, of a camp and tumuli. At the end there is a request to Astle to look into the heraldic visitations of Berkshire for confirmation of the grant of a coat of arms to a man whom Hasted claimed as his great-great-grandfather and lastly the historian begs for any material that either Astle, or Sir Joseph Ayloffe, or Dr. Ducarel may have relating to Kent. In reply Astle writes as follows:

Dear Sir,

Your obliging letter gave me a great pleasure. I shd. have answered it sooner but I was in hopes of giving you a satisfactory answer to your queries relating to your Pedigree. I have searched 5 several Visitations of Berks in the Br. Museum without success. I have since written to Mr. Bigland, Somerset Herald, who is my particular friend but I have not yet rec. an answer. I have discovered some materials relating to Kent, which, if I know you rightly, will be very agreeable to you; and what is more, I have a promise of the loan of them for your use.

I know you are burning with impatience to hear what those important materials are. Therefore know you that I have discovered a MS. history of Dover Castle written Temp Eliz. & Several drawings of the principal churches, castles, &c. in the County of Kent very accurately taken by Mr. Grove, a Gent. who takes views for his own amusement, & who is an excellent draughtsman. Pray inform me how I can convey these draughts to you & they shall be sent very soon.

I have found several things in the Aug. Office which will be very useful to you, but more of these hereafter. The Records there are of the highest importance to the public. I hope to see you at Surrenden at Xmas.

I presume you have the paper regularly; therefore it wd. be impertinent in me to give you the news of the Town. I have attended the House every day since the Session began.

Mr. Wilkes is not in any danger from his wound, tho. his fever is increased to-day. Last night he dictated a North Brit which contains a parallel bet. Lord Sandwich and himself. His essay on Woman is a most blasphemous & infamous libel, and strikes at the very roots of our most holy religion. That great pattern of virtue Lord Sandwich was very much enraged at this infamous piece & declared himself the champion of religion. He show'd the frontispiece to the whole House. It contained *magnus priapus erectus* with these words underneath σωτηρ κοσμου [Saviour of the world]. A figure of the B.V. with part of a verse from the 8th Iliad beneath επει ου σεο κυντερον αλλο *Quoniam non aliud te impudentius* [since there is nothing more impudent than you].

A friend of mine hath lately given me an account of a Pretorian edict in the time of Adrian lately found near Sheffield in Yorkshire. On the reverse are some characters which my friend takes to be Coptic, but he must certainly be mistaken. I think they are Runic. This edict is engraved upon a square brass plate about 18 inches by 12.

Last night Sir Jos. the Doctor & I attended at the Society of Antiquaries to propose you, & to ballot for Mr. Lloyd who was duly elected. The old

knight hath never been at a loss for a Toast since he saw Miss Wilkes; he
speaks of her in raptures.

> If Jenny's matchless charms do really move
> Old age, & frozen impotence to love,
> What must be my situation?

However, (joking apart) pray make my complimts. acceptable to that
most amiable lady. After mentioning Miss W. I have not one idea of
antiquity, & I think it wd. be absolutely absurd in me to descend to any
other subject, except it be to desire you will present my complimts. to
your good lady, and be assured that I remain, Dear Sir, Your obliged &
obdt. hble. servt. THOS ASTLE

Br. Museum
19th Novr. 1763

    When I hear from the Heralds Office I hope I shall be able to give you
some account of the ped. you desire. Pray excuse my inaccuracies; I am
now talking to 3 ladies who are just come here for the evening.

The first paragraph of this letter leaves no doubt as to its being an answer to that
of Hasted dated 15 days earlier.

    By the time Astle wrote his second letter he had received two more from Hasted,
written, like the first, from Throwley, near Faversham, where Hasted owned a
manor house which he seems to have used as a summer residence. When acknow-
ledging Astle's earlier letter Hasted observes that he is so infrequently in London
that he will not be able to take advantage of Astle's offers of access to the central
records:

>   I do assure you I work very hard from morning to night, and I have
> the good luck to have some very valuable MSS. pour in frequently. I have
> just finished the materials Dr. Plot left for his *Natural History of Kent,*
> and am now about those which Warburton, Somt. Herald, had collected
> for a history of this County.
>   I shall be very glad to wait on you, if you come to Surrenden at Xmas.
> Besides the pleasure I shall have in seeing you I shall have an opportunity
> of seeing the Surrenden library, for tho' I was very well acquainted with
> the late Sr. Edwd. Dering, I am not all known to the present gentn. One
> thing I enjoy much here, which induces me to stay at Throwley, I enjoy
> my time & leisure without the interruption of too many visitors, with
> which I was pestered at Sutton.

    Surrenden is near Pluckley, on the borders of the Weald of Kent; only a
fragment remains of this seat of the Derings, who for centuries were one of the
leading, and richest, families in Kent.

Before Astle could reply Hasted wrote again concerned mainly with the storm
in the antiquarian teacup that arose when Bryan Faussett went to the Society of
Antiquaries just when a letter from Hasted was being read out which gave a
description of Faussett's own excavations. The latter 'desired the president to

to pay no further regard to it and promised to send a true account of it'. Hasted tried to justify his letter to the Antiquaries and then gave some account of his progesss with the *History*:

> I work so hard at my favorite design, morning, noón, and night, that I know nothing of the world, but what my correspondents & the newspapers inform me of. I hope to do so much this winter in the transcribing part, that when the fine weather comes in summer I shall have nothing to prevent my visiting every parish in the county without which I can never compleat my work, and I should be very unwilling to print it before I had made use of your kind offers of the Augmentation Office & Museum, for which I must allot 4 or 5 months in London, but when that can be I cannot fix, as my materials increase beyond my utmost expectations, and tho' the further I proceed the more labour I find still to go thro', yet I am more & more convinced every day, that I shall be able to make it a history tolerably compleat; at least infinitely (more) so than any yet made public.

On 26 January Astle wrote again as follows:

Dear Sir,

I recd. yours of the 17th inst. which gave me great pleasure as it hath enabled me to desire the Society to suspend their judgments till they see Mr. Fosset's [*sic*] account. That part of your Letr. only, which related to the Roman Camp was read, and it was so acceptable to the Society that it was ordered to be read at the next meeting. They observed they were glad they had elected so communicative a member. I took the liberty of making one trifling alteration, and I am sure the style and diction of your Ltr. is very clear, nervous & descriptive, and such as might be read before any Society in England. I was not at the Society when your account of the Camp was read a second time, and when Mr. Fosset made his observations upon it, but I am now going there and shall inform the Society that I know you are incapable of asserting an untruth; that the description is not only just, but the conjectures are such as Mr. F. acquiesced in at the time when you viewed the encampment. Therefore I shall desire them to suspend their judgments till Mr. F. sends the promis'd account.

I am glad to hear that you make such great progress in your *History of Kent.* Sir Joseph & I have been no less assiduous at the Augmentation Office. Our calendars (which I hope you will take the benefit of) will amaze you.[1]

The Gent. who hath the drawings says he will make copies of any of them for you but as they were all taken by himself, & he sets a great value upon them, he is unwilling to part with them out of his custody. The account of Dover Castle he will send to me at any time. I have lately purchased an original Treaty of Peace between O. Cromwell & John IV. King of Portugal which I have given to Mr. Grenville. I have also purchsd. an original Register of Worcester Priory, beginning Ao. 963 & ending Ao. 1240; in this Regr. is entered the famous chre of King Edgar the or. of which is in the Harl. Library No. 7513 which Dr. Hickes (in his

Thos. Lit. Septentrion p. 86 & at fol. 152 of the Dissertatis Epistolaris) says is a forgery; perhaps so, but if it is forged, the forgery is very ancient for it is entered in this book Ao. 1133 temp. H 1.

But my greatest discovery is at Peterchurch in Wales. A friend of mine who is made engineer at Milford Haven, informs me that in sinking a foundation for a Fort they found a cavern in the rock in the middle of which was a leaden box in which was contained a roll of very strong leather (which the Welsh take to be wolf skins). Upon it is written, in the old square character, a part of the history of Cadwallader, the British hero. I hope to give you a better account of this MS. soon as I have some thoughts of having the original sent to me in London. I have made several notes for you relating to Kent which I will transmit to you as soon as I conveniently can. I am with complmts. to your Lady, and to Miss W., if she is with you, Dear Sir, Yours faithful hble sert. THOS. ASTLE

Br. Museum
26th Jany. 1764

Sir Joseph Ayliffe who is now with me thinks the skins are likely to be buffallow as those beasts abounded in Wales formerly.

His complmts. attend you; Dr. Ducarel is well. Pray let me hear from you soon.

The only real interest in Hasted's long-delayed reply is in the postscript:

As it is impossible to be an antiquarian without having a particular attachment to the ladies, at least I judge so, from those I have the pleasure of being acquainted with, and you are a young man, why cannot you take a ride to our Assize Ball, Wednesday sennight; if you are fond of dancing you will have an exceeding good one, and in all likelihood your flame will be there. I would induce you if I could in the first place for your own sake & in the next, that I may have the pleasure of meeting you there. I don't question if you were to give Sir Joseph two or three items of our Kentish lasses, if he would not leave even the charms of the British Museum for those of a beautifull lass of seventeen. Adieu.

The anonymous editor of the Hasted–Astle letters remarks that 'Hasted was evidently fully alive to the value of Astle's friendship, and his advances seem to have been met with considerable generosity, though judging from the single extant letter in reply from his pen, Astle's correspondence was not marked by the same effusiveness'. This guess is now seen to be wide of the mark.

In the first letter the abrupt and unexpected switch, without any prefatory remark, to Mr. Wilkes almost suggests that the latter was a mutual acquaintance. The wound must have been the one received in Wilkes' famous duel with Samuel Martin, and some of Astle's remarks must be taken as being ironical; Sandwich, 'that great pattern of virtue', was a former associate of Wilkes in his indecent and blasphemous activities at Medmenham Abbey. And who is this 'Miss Wilkes', apparently staying with the Hasteds? One more is added to our list of minor mysteries, to be tackled sooner or later.

Thorpe, John (1715–92)

A great Kent antiquary as was his father of the same name. The father compiled and the son published *Registrum Roffense,* the name given to a collection of manuscripts, inscriptions, etc., relating to Rochester. Thorpe seems to have been a close friend of the historian and encouraged him in the face of adverse criticism.

The letters of John Thorpe all came from Bexley and some of them mention his address, High Street House, which still stands. The first of any note is dated 2 June 1775, and concerns an estate in North Cray about which Thorpe was obviously trying to find out a few facts at Hasted's request: 'I have been fishing among the N. Cray folks, who cannot inform me of the names of the gentlemen married to two of the miss Broke's'. Thorpe thanks Hasted for his invitation to visit Canterbury but continues 'I am heartily sorry I can't embrace the Doctor's kind offer but we go the beginning of July to Penshurst and tarry 'till the latter end of August, a visit which we make every other year to our friends there'.

This sounds very much like the world of Jane Austen, and presumably the 'Doctor'—possibly Ducarel—had offered the Thorpes a lift to Canterbury. When he is at Penshurst, Thorpe offers to correct some of Hasted's maps 'as my friend Mr. Wakefield is a Commissioner of the Turnpikes there and perfectly well acquainted with all the roads, etc., in that part of the county'. It appears that the engraver Bayly was entrusted with the drawing of these maps and Thorpe remarks:

> I have taken the liberty to correct for our friend Bayly many omissions and mistakes that have come within the compass of my knowledge in the hundreds of the Lath of Sutton, for though he is an able artist yet we may say with Horace he is *abnormis sapiens* in matters of this kind, not having the Kentish historians, etc., to direct him. He has got my Kilburne which he says is of great service to him as to the names of the parishes and proper divisions of the hundreds.

Richard Kilburne (1605–78) published a *Topography or Survey or Kent.* This passage well illustrates the rough and ready methods that were used to prepare Hasted's maps.

On 9 October 1775 Thorpe is writing about the estates of the Sidney family who then, as now, held Penshurst Place. We can contrast Thorpe's lively account with Hasted's cold and factual mixture of legalism and genealogy. The estate had found its way into the hands of female co-heirs and one half-share had gone to Lady Mary Sidney Sherard, the other to Mrs. Elizabeth Perry (*née* Sidney). Wrote Thorpe

> Lady Sherard being entitled to one-half of the Sydney Estates, even of the furniture, pictures, etc., in the great house, at her death Mr. Weston, Sr. G. Yonge's Steward, went down and numbered with white paint every oak on the estates, and in the park, so that Mrs. Perry was obliged to sell & mortgage some part of her own moiety, amounting, as 'tis said, to the sum of two, or three and twenty thousand pounds, to have the fine old seat, park and manor of Penshurst to herself. I was present at the sale of Lady Yonge's moiety of the family pictures at Langford's, when Mrs. Perry herself bought most of them in again: a heartbreaking task, no doubt, by having the estates so torn to pieces and divided through her

sister Sherrard's disaffection in leaving her moiety from herself &
children to Lady Yonge, who was no relation. It is too often the misfortune for unnatural relations to leave their estates to strangers. I
speak feelingly, and from experience, having like Mrs. Perry been a
sufferer in that parish.

Thorpe then tells how a member of his own family had willed to strangers estates
which Thorpe's father had expected to inherit.

Hasted relates quite baldly that Lady Mary Sherard bequeathed her interests to
Lady Yonge and her son and that 'they in the year 1770 joined in the sale of the
undivided moiety of the Sidney estates to Mrs. Elizabeth Perry, of Penshurst Place,
the present possessor of these estates'.

Again Thorpe criticises Bayly who, he says, 'is certainly a most dilatory creature
& requires good spurring; which I will give him as you desire'. As well as answering
Hasted's queries, Thorpe seems to have made it his particular province to assist in
the maps and plates. Not only does he mention repeatedly the need to spur Bayly
on to produce quicker results, but he is prolific in suggestions as to who might be
approached to provide (gratis, of course) plates of gentlemen's seats and other
noteworthy buildings. A letter of January 1776 deals at some length with Bromley
College and names a rich benefactor who might be induced to contribute a picture
of it. Some of Thorpe's suggestions seem to have borne fruit and a plate of the
college adorns Folio I. The edifice survives to this day and is described in the West
Kent and Weald volume in the 'Buildings of England' series; one can therefore
bridge the centuries by comparing Bayly's engraving of the college with John
Newman's account of it. For an engraving of Wye College in East Kent Thorpe
suggests an approach to 'the present Lord Mayor', who has a seat in that parish.[2]
'Mrs. Perry may be prevailed on to present a plate of Penshurst Place and the Duke
of Dorset perhaps would contribute Knoll [sic]; Cobham Hall likewise would be a
noble print, but who has interest with Lord Darnley I know not.'

The first volume of the *History* was not to appear for another two years, but
Thorpe says: 'I am often asked if your work is in the press. If it was known it would
be a means of hastening the subscriptions', and adds: 'I hope you will excuse all
my above rambling hints, as flowing from a hearty well wisher to you'.

In March 1777 Thorpe acknowledges a letter from Hasted describing it as 'an
unexpected favour' and proceeds to upbraid the historian for his long silence;
'I imagined you had forgot an old friend and dropped his correspondence'. However, he forgives Hasted on the grounds of the 'great fatigue' caused by 'arduous
and laborious work'. The attack on Bayly's dilatoriness is resumed, with the
promise that on his next visit to Town Thorpe will administer 'a smart spur' to
the engraver who 'requires now and then a good jogging'. We learn of a quarrel
between Hasted and 'the Doctor' (perhaps Dr. Ducarel), for which Thorpe
administers a reproof:

Friends should never suffer their tempers to be ruffled by heats and
animosities. We are to forget and forgive one anothers faults; and I will
make it my business to see the Dr. and endeavour to conciliate this
unhappy affair.

Thorpe lists the gentlemen's seats in the parish of Bexley and, at Hasted's request one may suppose, gives an account of his own house, which had earlier belonged to a branch of the Austen family. The title is traced back to Sir Robert Austen in the 17th century. The house replaces an older one pulled down in 1761.

The next letter of interest (25 November 1778) begins as follows:

> I am glad to hear, by your kind favour of the 16th instant, that you have begun printing your second volume and will favour the public with a third, which will enable you to treat more fully of your city & its district, for Gostling has slovened over the other religious houses, &c., confining himself chiefly to the Cathedral & its environs.

'Gostling' is Canon William Gostling, whose well-loved book *A Walk in and About the City of Canterbury* went through several editions. The Canon was already dead when the usually kindly Thorpe made this not very complimentary remark. He complains again of Hasted's neglect but excuses him on account of the 'constant hurry and confusion of business you are immersed in', and asks Hasted to insert his name 'in the list of your friends in the second volume':

> When it is finished I shall bind the books handsomely and insert the General Map in the first volume. You need be in no hurry about my MS. papers, but at any time when you see your son, or convey any parcel to him in town it will be time enough.

Thorpe next refers to a 'capital' sale of the lands, goods, stock and implements of husbandry of one Thomas Edsall, whose failure he thinks can be put down to extravagance:

> Had he been content with his mills and house there, and followed that business close he might have accumulated a noble fortune; but what fortune can support luxury and extravagance? Instead of minding business he has been taking every step since his father's death to ruin himself. His house in Cannon Street and two in the country, all compleatly furnished, with a chariot, phaeton, two whiskys, a fine sailing vessel which cost £500 and the charge of keeping it £200 p. ann., besides its furnishings with provisions, parties of pleasure in it &c.

Thorpe does not hesitate to reveal his small respect for the denizens of cathedral closes: 'You know I look upon Deans & Chapter in the same light that you do, and wish that Government would lay a good tax upon them, and ease the laity'. Thorpe discloses one of his favourite hobbies and asks Hasted to pass a message to 'Friend Dix', 'that I mutually wished for him to be a partaker of the sport when I was angling, and shall be glad if he will come and throw a fly with me in the summer'. We are reminded that fly-fishing is no modern invention.

From a letter of June 1779 we learn that Thorpe's daughter is soon to be married:

> My best thanks are due for your most kind & friendly letter, together with my daughter's compliments for your obliging and sincere wishes for her welfare in the matrimonial state. Nothing can add more to her happiness

than the good opinion of her friends, among whom she justly esteems
Mr. & Mrs. Hasted. The gentleman she is going to marry is Mr. Meggison,
an eminent attorney in Grays-Inn, a man of fortune, family & good
connexions; and I think there is a fair prospect of all conjugal felicity.
He has taken a handsome house in Hatton-Garden, which is now furnish-
ing for them; and where they will be glad to see Mr. & Mrs. Hasted when
they come to Town, & will do them that pleasure. As the wedding will be
sometime next month, & as you are so very kind to postpone your visit
to us this summer on account of the bustle, you say we may be in, we
shall therefore hope for that pleasure the next; when you may then
be more at leisure, from the great fatigue & close application to your
work.

Thorpe then gives an account of the estate of Nettlested in Stockbury, which
he has inherited from his father:

> Nettlested, now a farm-house, is seated on the east side of Stockbury
> Street; & was for many generations the mansion house and residence of
> the Plotts, ancestors of the learned *Historiographer* Robt. Plott, LL.D. &
> Register of the Court of Chivalry and Keeper of the Ashmolean Museum.
> Of the two 1st places the original patents of his creation signed by King
> James 2d. & Hen. Duke of Norfolk in my possession.

After tracing the ownership of the estate to Thomas Thurstone, who sold it to
his father, Thorpe writes:

> The above is a fair account of my property in that parish; which brings
> it down to my time, and please to insert in your Hist. as I intend to sell
> it, being at a great distance from me, and the only estate in that part of
> the county; as part of my daughter's portion. You are sensible girls
> nowadays don't go to market without money. Your son dined with me
> lately; and Mr. Wills spent a day's fishing with me a fortnight ago.

The name of Rowe Mores was completely unknown to me until I read Thorpe's
letter of 5 February 1781. After some pleasantries, he writes:

> No doubt you have seen Mr. More's excellent and well drawn Hist. of
> the Parish of Tunstall, which may be of some service to you in your work.
> It is published in the 1st. No. of the *Bibliotheca Topographica Britannica,*
> a work which will be ably conducted and supported. The 1st No. is five
> shillings; the 2nd & 3rd will soon be published. It will be very expensive,
> but I can't forbear taking in these kind of antiquarian publications.
> Notwithstanding More's Hist. has such merit, which may be easily under-
> taken for any single or separate parish; yet to pursue his plan in a large
> County Hist. Good Lord! how voluminous would it be, and what few
> could purchase it, or indeed, what man's life or pocket is adequate to
> it? Therefore the Editors might have spared their severe censure on
> your Hist. in the last page of their preface.

Questionnaires, Thorpe points out, covering so large an area as a complete county
would almost certainly be for the most part ignored: 'I only mention the above

that you may, if you think proper, vindicate yourself and give these carpers a dressing in your next preface' Here was another essential task—running to earth a copy of this critical article.

A month later, however, Thorpe, after supplying more detail about Stockbury and Nettlested, ends, 'As to the critics, I think you judge right to take no notice and despise them'.

Of Thorpe's last significant letter only a part remains; it is fairly clear that the missing piece referred to some embarrassing family topic. After the part torn away, the letter continues:

> . . . and should Dingley, or anyone, mention it I shall only say that young men nowadays prefer the Army or Navy to serving in a shop. I am glad you go on with your *History*; and pray keep up your spirits, and trust to Providence: so I shall dwell no longer on this unpleasant subject.

Potter, John (1713-70)

The following is a letter from the Rev. John Potter, rector and vicar of Wrotham, between Sevenoaks and Maidstone:

> I applied some time since to Dr. Ducarell to beg that he would give me such intelligence as he might happen to pick up with regard to the Lands, Privileges and Immunities of the Knights of St John of Jerusalem; in answer to this he acquainted me that you have an account of all their possessions in Kent, and (*inter alia*) a terrier of their Lands in Wrotham, and that you were so kind as to say you would be ready upon my application to give me any information in your power. At your leisure therefore I would intreat the favour of you to copy out and to sent me only a short extract of any account which you have of their possessions, &c., in my Parish of Wrotham. Or if they are too long or otherwise difficult to be copied I would take some opportunity of waiting upon you at Sutton when I am in that part of the country, and examine with you the papers relating to them. I hope your conferences with Mr. Whitworth will enable you together to make a perfect continuation and a good new edition of Philpot;[3] I think the method of publishing alphabetically as soon as you have a few of the first letters complete will be attended with ease and satisfaction to yourselves and the publick, and perhaps it may induce some of those whose names or properties are concerned under each letter to send you further instructions.
>
> I shall be very ready, if it should fall in my way to collect and to give you any intelligence that may be useful, or to answer any questions which you shall find occasion to direct to me at Canterbury or at Lydd in Kent.
>
> I am, Sr. Your most obedt. servt.   J. POTTER
>
> Canterbury.   July 10th, 1763.

This letter may seem of little interest until we learn something of its background. John Potter was the elder son of an Archbishop of Canterbury of the same name (1674-1747). John junior was disinherited by his class-conscious father (himself the son of a linen-draper) for marrying an Oxford University bedmaker. John's birthright went to his younger brother, Thomas, who was thereby enabled to embark upon a political career and to become an associate of the elder Pitt. It is one of fate's little ironies that this beneficiary of a prelate's social sensitivity was, in his looser moments, a prominent member of the Medmenham sect of practitioners of lechery and devil-worship, and was the reputed author of perhaps the most indecent and blasphemous document in the language, the *Essay on Woman*. It is more pleasant to relate that his elder brother managed to secure before he died the valuable deanery of Canterbury, and that the Dean and the erstwhile college domestic are buried together in the Cathedral Cloisters.

John's letter provides us with a piece of information about the plan for a second edition of Philipott's *Villare Cantianum* not recorded elsewhere.

Thomas Secker (1693–1768)

It would scarcely be appropriate to omit from the selection two letters from another Archbishop of Canterbury, Thomas Secker, which Hasted must have preserved amongst the materials of his *History* out of respect for the writer rather than for any information that they contained. He seems to have taken very seriously his position as Squire of Huntingfold in Throwley, and did not hesitate to beard the archbishop himself if he detected any shortcomings in the ecclesiastical administration of the parish. The archbishop writes:

> I am very much obliged to you for both parts of your letter. Mr. Lawson represented to me that Throwley disagreed with his health, and that the Death of his Brother there had made it insupportable to him: and for these reasons I allowed him to serve Pluckley. But I told him that according to some information which I had received, Throwley was worth £100 a year and that if it were so, he ought, according to the Rule of my predecessor Archbishop Potter to have a resident curate there, who should perform the whole service. In answer to this he assured me that the whole income was not £85 a year. And as I had mentioned to him that he had an estate, he assured me that by reason of incumbrances on it his present income from it was very little. On these considerations I allowed him to take Mr. Dawney for his curate, with a salary of £25 a year: and the rather, as I understood, that Mr. Dawney could not easily get another curacy, and yet stood in need of one. I did not know that his health was bad: and on knowing it now from you, am in a great difficulty between concern for him and for the parish of Throwley. I hope you and the other parishioners will be content to bear some inconveniences on his account; yet I would not desire more from you than is reasonable. And I shall be very glad to know your second thoughts, after reading this state of the case, as it hath been represented to me.
>
> It will be a great pleasure to me if the Library here can afford you any entertainment. I return you my thanks for the sight of the manuscript of Archbishop Laud's sequestred revenue, and the allowance made to him out of it for his maintenance in the Tower. And if you will be so good as to let me have copies of any papers in your hands, relative to

church matters, and particularly to the See of Canterbury, it will be esteemed a great favour by

Your faithful servant   THOS. CANT.

Lambeth.   Nov. 12th, 1763.

Since I received the favour of your last letter Mr. Lawson hath given me in writing an account of every particular article of the income of Throwley, by which it amounts to £84 6s. 4½d. besides £6 6s. 0d. for the house and some small pieces of ground. Now I do not in other cases require the whole service for livings under £100 a year, and therefore cannot equitably require it in this case. He hath also given me an account of his temporal income, according to which, when deductions are made for reserved rent renewals, taxes, repairs, annuitants and money borrowed at interest, the clear income to him, since his mother's death, is not £84 a year. I have pressed him very much, both formerly and now, to reside at Throwley. He assures me it hath never agreed with his health, and is become so melancholy a place to him, on several accounts, that he cannot bear it. Therefore, as he is an infirm and splenetick man, I am afraid to urge him any further. Mr. Dawney represented to me some time ago that with the curacy of Throwley he could but barely maintain himself. And therefore, if he quits that, he must have some other, unless he be unfit for any: of which I never had any intimation before, but shall inquire concerning it. At present I neither know where any other provision can be made for him nor for the parish of Throwley. For it is extremely difficult everywhere to get curates. I shall be glad to settle everything to your satisfaction as far and as soon as I can. But in the meantime that you, who set so good an example in all other respects, will not set the bad one of absenting yourself from the publick service is the earnest request of

Your faithful servant   THOS. CANT.

Lambeth.   Dec. 9th, 1763.

Dacre, Lord (fl. 1768-82)

His family name was Lennard and they held Chevening before the Stanhopes. The most famous Lennard was Francis, the 14th Baron, who was prominent on the parliamentary side in the Civil War. The former Lennard seat was offered as a residence for the Prince of Wales. Lord Dacre contributed voluminously concerning Chevening and the Lennard family. The last letter in this selection comes from him, writing in August 1778 from Belhouse, near Greys in Essex. For the reason he gives only the signature and the last part of the postscript are in Dacre's own shaky hand:

Sir,

The rheumatism which I at present have in my hand, enough to give me pain to write, will I hope plead my excuse with you for making use of a friend's; as I would lose no time in thanking you for the fine copy you have favored me with, of your *History of Kent,* which I have this day received. I have, as you desired, enquired the name of the engraver of

Miss Lennard's Plate, which is I. Caldwell, who lives in Windmill Street the top of the Haymarket; and the reason he assigns for not putting his name is that he is not used to engrave writing but has it done by another, so I understand that between them the name was omitted. If however, were it thought material for his name to appear, on sending him the copper Plate he would get it inserted.

And now I must say a word or two about the account in your Book of my family (which I naturally first turned to) and where unluckily by some oversight there are some material mistakes in the very beginning of it, and even anachronisms; page 359 column 2nd 'tis said that 'Herbert Fitz-herbert by his deed and indenture July 18th in the fourth year of the above Reign (viz. of K. Ed. 6th) conveyed this manor (viz Chevening) and premises to John Lennard Esq. and his heirs who soon after in his brother William Lennard's name purchased the above rent of £20. John Lennard Gent. was *at that time* of Chevening and resided at Chepsted in this Parish. He left a son George who lived in the reign of King Henry the 7th and was of Chepsted'.

You will in the first place observe that you make John Lennard Gent. who lived at Chevening in Edwd. 6th's time father of George, who lived in the reign of King Henry the 7th, and further the order of the descent is here inverted, for George Lennard was the father and John Lennard Gentleman was the son, which John Lennard married Anne, daughter of Thomas Bird in the time of King Edw. the 6th, for it appears by the epitaph upon the tomb of his son John Lennard Gent. in Chevening church that he (the son) was born the 19th of Ed. 4th, for so, if his age (as there marked) be computed backward, it will be found.

To correct therefore the aforesaid errors; the account of the Lennard family beginning the 23rd line from the top should run as follows; and which all the records and pedigrees of the family universally agree in:

'This family was settled here at Chevening as early at least as K. Hen. the 6th time, when we find George Lennard then living there, who by Maud his wife had issue John his son and heir, who by Anne, daughter and heir of Thoms. Bird of Middx., had issue 3 sons, John born 19th Ed. the 4th of whom hereafter, etc. etc. etc'. for the rest of the 31st line and all after it is right.

I own, dear sir, that both for the perfectness of the work and on my own account I wish that these errors might not stand so in your book; especially as the account is said in a note to be taken entirely from *my* papers. Could not therefore this sheet be *re*printed, corrected as above, and circulated amongst the subscribers etc. as I have known done in similar cases. As to any extraordinary expence that this may be attended with, I would not wish to burthen you with it, but would willingly take it upon myself. I will here just add that the pedigree from George Lennard as I have given it you is confirmed by Phillpot's Stemmata in off Arm: Liley Rouge Croix's pedigrees of the nobility temp. James 1st penes Com. de Egmont Visit of Kent anno 1619 in the Harleian collection No. 1588 and the epitaph of Catharine Lennard in Hethfield church (*sic*), and a pedigree in the handwriting of my ancestor Sampson Lennard Esq. of Chevening.

After having so long trespassed on you I will take up no more of your time at present only to beg your acceptance of half a buck which I shall take the first opportunity of sending you by the Canterbury coach, and of which I will give you timely notice by a line.

I am, Sir, with great regard, Your obdt. hble. servt.

DACRE

Belhouse near Grays
Augt. 3rd 1778

Postscript. I must on recollection further observe to you that in the 35th line of said column p. 359 the word (daughter) should be (sister).

Also in the 42nd line instead of Blue Mantle Pursuivant I could wish these words were put 'in the wars in the Low Country *with Sir Philip Sidney'*. The note will show that he was of the College of Arms.

Also page 360 line 3 instead of *industry* to put *abilities.* For he really deserves this epithet and you would say so if you saw the letters of his which I have.

There are some puzzling features. Dacre has received a 'fine copy' of the first volume of the *History* but discovers some 'material mistakes' in the account of his family, the Lennards, in the article on Chevening. Having set out the precise amendments required, he insists that the relevant sheet (a sheet comprised four pages) be reprinted, and the corrected copy circulated amongst the subscribers. In a later letter he resisted a suggestion that a correction in the Errata would be good enough. The difficulty is to understand how alterations could be made, even on lordly instruction, in a book already published. It was therefore of interest to find out what exactly appeared in the book as it has come down to us. The two copies in the Canterbury Cathedral library were found to comply exactly in their texts with Lord Dacre's suggestions. Most conspicuously, there is nothing about Sampson Lennard's being Bluemantle Pursuivant. However, on my returning home and similarly checking my own copy of the *History* I made a discovery which, I must admit, gave me no little pleasure and satisfaction: in my book Sampson Lennard *was* Bluemantle Pursuivant, and the other passages which Dacre criticised could also be read in their original form. The only explanation for this startling discovery seemed to be that the *History* was issued in some unbound or lightly bound state in which it was still possible to remove one or more of the printer's sheets and substitute other ones before the book was permanently bound. The discovery would be less important if my own copy was a single freak, rather like a postage stamp with the head upside-down. But the fact that even one copy of the first edition of *Hasted* had a different text seemed to be an important discovery to make a couple of centuries after the publication of the volume.

It was, it seems, a not uncommon practice in the 18th century for books published by subscription to be issued unbound, and Thorpe's remark, in one of his letters, that he would bind Hasted's books handsomely, was confirmation that this must have been Hasted's practice. It was therefore possible to replace a faulty text so long as the owner had not yet had the book bound. As a result of my discovery I have made it a practice to check any copies of the *History* that I come across; so far the corrected and uncorrected copies are running almost neck and neck, so my book is not a mere freak. The most distinguished holders of an uncorrected, or 'Bluemantle', copy are the Kent County Archives Office!

Many of the letters on Hasted's files, though themselves of no great interest, come from interesting people. The section which follows gives some biographical information about these correspondents and a brief idea of the way in which they helped the historian.

Biographies of Correspondents

Amherst, Jeffrey, Baron Amherst of Holmesdale (1717–97)

Was Wolfe's Commander-in-Chief in the conquest of Canada and himself captured Louisburg, Cape Breton, Ticonderoga and Montreal. He retired to a seat in Sevenoaks which he named Montreal; the house has gone, but there is still a district called Montreal Park. Amherst's account of his own military successes was transcribed almost word for word by Hasted.

Astle, Thomas (1735–1803)

Perhaps Hasted's principal mentor. Astle held at one time or another some of the most important posts connected with the care of the public records of the kingdom, and his advice was constantly sought by the government of the day on such matters; he became Keeper of the Records in the Tower of London and a trustee of the British Museum, and wrote an important book on the subject of palaeography.

Austen, Francis (fl. 1777)

Clerk of the Peace of Kent, living at Sevenoaks, and man-of-business to the Duke of Dorset. He was a great-uncle of the novelist Jane Austen and supplied Hasted with much useful information about the different places in West Kent.

Banks, Sir Joseph (1734–1820)

Sailed with Captain Cook as botanist on the voyage of the *Endeavour* to the Pacific (1769–71) and later became president of the Royal Society, which he ruled with a rod of iron. Though a patron of science rather than a worker, he nevertheless braved every danger on the voyage with Captain Cook in pursuit of botanical knowledge. He married a Hugessen heiress to inherit the picturesque seat of Provender, near Faversham, where Prince and Princess Romanoff lived until recently. Banks' letter is about his own adventures—at Hasted's request.

Bathurst, Richard (fl. 1775–98)

Lived at Finchcocks on the Sussex border, where his family had been since Tudor times. They had provided Oliver Cromwell with his physician and the 18th century with its worst Lord Chancellor. Richard, a kinsman of Mrs. Hasted, checked the historian's proofs relating to Goudhurst, and provided extra material which was not, however, used. It concerned the apocryphal activities in Goudhurst of two notorious characters—King Charles II and the Devil.

Beauvoir, Osmund (d. 1789)

Headmaster of the King's School, Canterbury, and has been described as the only noteworthy one between 1685 and 1832. He was, at the same time, it seems, vicar of Littlebourne, a short distance from Canterbury, and of Milton, near Sittingbourne. He was also one of the Six Preachers in Canterbury Cathedral and yet found time to help Hasted with details about tithes and such-like matters, and to assist Canon Gostling in composing his well-known *Walks about Canterbury*.

Boys, William (1735-1803)

In partnership with William Boteler, Boys was Hasted's main support in his task of producing the last volume of his *History* under great difficulties. The Boys were one of the most prominent families in Kent, with at least 17 recognisable branches in different parts of the county. Boasting of their Norman blood, their principal preoccupation was land-ownership, though the most active members sometimes aspired to a deanery or a minor naval or military command. At the end of the 18th century, however, they produced John, a well-known agricultural expert and sheep-breeder, and William, the subject of this note who wrote the standard history of Sandwich.

Brett, Nicholas (d. 1776)

Was the scion of a distinguished Kent family living at Wye, his father being a prominent non-juring divine who, in 1714, resigned his livings rather than take the oaths imposed by the government. The family seat was at Spring Grove, which still stands near the old Wye racecourse and is a private school for young boys. Brett loaned important and useful MSS. to Hasted and supplied information which is particularly interesting in that it was directed to bring up to date Philipott's *Villare Cantianum,* thus providing evidence that in his earlier stages Hasted had such a project in mind.

Brooke, John Charles (1748-94)

Somerset Herald and a Fellow of the Society of Antiquaries, Brooke supplied Hasted with pedigrees of Kent families. The most extraordinary thing about him was the manner of his death: he was crushed to death trying to get into the pit at the *Haymarket Theatre.*

Brydges, Sir Samuel Egerton (1762-1837)

Antiquarian, publisher and genealogist. In return for Brydges' help with pedigrees Hasted seems to have done some devilling for him in connection with the claim (rejected by the House of Lords) of his brother, Timewell Brydges, to the barony of Chandos.

Burnaby, Andrew (1734-1812)

In Hasted's *History* he had merely a mention as the vicar of Greenwich. From the historian's correspondence we find that Burnaby supplied details about property ownerships there and about tithes and the market. Hasted does not tell us that he was also Archdeacon of Leicester and a major landowner in that district and in Huntingdonshire. Before settling down to enjoy these advantages he had travelled in the American colonies, in Italy (where he was temporarily British Pro-Consul) and in Corsica where he became acquainted with the statesman Paoli. He published accounts of his adventures.

Burrell, Sir William (1732-96)

A lawyer practising at Doctors' Commons, Chancellor of two dioceses and M.P. for Haslemere, Sir William held besides a heterogeneous collection of ecclesiastical, legal and commercial appointments. For a time he owned the family estate in Beckenham, and it thus fell to him to brief Hasted as to the family's ownerships. The latter seems to have had some difficulty in sorting out the details—the accounts of the family in the first and second editions of the *History* seem to be somewhat at variance.

Cator, John (1730-1806)

The squire of Beckenham, whose old mansion is now a golf club-house. He receives a mention in Boswell, who relates that Johnson 'was pleased with the kindness of Mr. Cator, who was joined with him in Mr. Thrale's important trust', and thus describes him: 'There is much good in his character, and much usefulness in his knowledge'. He found a cordial solace at that gentleman's seat at Beckenham 'which is indeed one of the finest places at which I ever was a guest; and where I find more and more a hospitable welcome'. Cator offered to contribute a plate to the *History,* and one presumes the engravings of Beckenham Place was the result.

Children, George (1742-1818)

Landowner and banker in the Tonbridge area, who made pioneer electrical experiments in his spare time. His bank failed, and he died in poverty. However, his son, John George, carried on the scientific work of his father, associated with Sir Humphrey Davy, and became secretary of the Royal Society. The father provided some details about his estate at Cranbrook.

Darnley, Lord (1719-81)

The family name of Bligh and it was John, the third earl, who was Hasted's correspondent. The Blighs were an English family who had enriched themselves in Ireland; they had no connection with the Lord Darnley who was married to Mary Queen of Scots. The Kentish Lord Darnley is remarkable for the freedom with which he criticised the text of Hasted's article on Cobham, which he seems to have seen in proof, and his even more scathing denunciation of the impression of his seat Cobham Hall by the engraver Bayly, which the noble lord had, rashly as he afterwards felt, agreed to pay for.

Davis, Sir John (d. 1766)

Provides a link with the famed topographer of Kent, Richard Kilburne (1605-78). Davis gave Hasted some details about the burial of Kilburne, his great-grandfather, in whose former house he himself now lived. This was Fowlers, at Hawkhurst, and Fowlers Park commemorates the name to this day.

Deedes, William (senior) (d. 1793) and junior (fl. 1799)

There have been many men of this name in the history of Kent down to the present editor of the *Daily Telegraph,* The Rt. Hon. William Francis Deedes. At the time Hasted was writing, the Deedes, based on Hythe, were engaged in acquiring estates in many parishes in East Kent, and by 1799 William Deedes (jr.) had begun to build the family seat at Sandling Park. The estates were lost after the Wall Street crash in 1929 and the mansion, having been transferred to a relation of the family, was hit by a German bomb in World War II and ultimately had to be demolished, being replaced by a smaller, austerely modern building.

Denne, Samuel (1730-99)

The son of an archdeacon, Samuel Denne was for many years vicar of Wilmington, near Dartford, not far from Hasted's home during the early years of his marriage. The two were on familiar terms, and Denne's letters to Hasted contain much local gossip as well as information needful for the *History*. A quiet and studious man, Samuel Denne was, like his father before him, a keen antiquarian and wrote about the history of Lambeth and of Rochester.

Disney, William, D.D. (1731-1807)

The information that the vicar of Pluckley, William Disney, provided was noteworthy in various ways. In his parish was Surrenden, the ancestral home of the great Dering family, of whom Disney supplied a pedigree. He was Hasted's informant for both the first and the second editions of the *History*; significantly, his contribution to the latter included for the first time a description of the parish. Before settling down as a country parson, Disney had had a brilliant academic career at Cambridge, where he was Senior Wrangler, Regius Professor of Hebrew, and a Fellow of his college. The creator of 'Disneyland' was of the same ancient family.

Ducarel, Andrew Coltee (1713-85)

Librarian of Lambeth Palace. Secretary to five archbishops. Toured the country studying antiquities, and married his maid out of gratitude for her nursing him through an illness. He died of shock on hearing she was at the point of death which proved to be incorrect. He was one of Hasted's principal mentors.

Fairfax, Thomas, 6th Baron (1692-1782)

Appears in the Hasted story only by proxy, the historian's queries about his family and estates being answered by Denny Martin, the son of Lord Fairfax's brother-in-law, and curate of Leeds (Kent). Fairfax was an important figure in the history of America. He resided there from about 1747, having inherited from his wife's family the Colepepers of Greenway Court, vast estates in Virginia, as well as Leeds Castle in Kent. George Washington, when a youth, was Fairfax's protégé. In his home at Greenway Court, Virginia, Fairfax heard the news of the downfall at Yorktown of the British caused by the hand of his erstwhile pupil, and the blow killed him.

Farmer, Richard, D.D. (1735–97)

Was master of Emmanuel College, Cambridge, before occupying the ninth Prebend at Canterbury. A character if ever there was one. Farmer loved above all else old port, old clothes and old books, and could never be persuaded to get up in the morning, to go to bed at night, or to pay a bill. His essay on *The Learning of Shakespeare* showed the Bard had not a great deal of that commodity.

Faussett, Bryan (1720–76) and Henry Godfrey (b. 1749)

Henry was Bryan's eldest son. Hasted knew them both and borrowed the father's copy of Harris's *History of Kent* on which the owner had made manuscript notes. Bryan was a lightning operator in excavating sepulchral barrows and graves in Kent. His collection of grave goods was allowed to go to Liverpool. Hasted got into hot water for reporting to the Society of Antiquaries on Bryan's excavations instead of leaving it to the archaeologist to do himself. Henry Godfrey fed Hasted with much information about antiquities and family estates in the Nackington area.

Fawkes, Francis (1720–77)

Poet and translator of classical authors, praised by Dr. Johnson. Turned his talent also to drinking songs, one of which, 'The Brown Jug', became a classic. His jolly, sociable character did not, however, help him to advance in the church beyond the rectory of Hayes, and he died a poor man. His knowledge of the Orpington and Hayes districts was of assistance to Hasted.

Filmer, Sir John (1737–97)

Although he resided at the well-known seat of East Sutton Place, his correspondence with Hasted concerns the parish of Crundale in quite another part of Kent. History tells us nothing about this gentleman's own activities, but three other members of his family are recorded, two on the roll of fame and the other on a tablet of brass. Sir Robert (d. 1653) was a royalist political writer who had his house plundered 10 times and was imprisoned in Leeds Castle for his views, and his grandson Edward (b. 1657) was a dramatist of some repute. The father of Sir Robert (another Edward) who died in 1629 is commemorated by a large and well-preserved funerary brass in East Sutton church.

Foote, Francis Hender (d. 1773)

Owner of Charlton Place, Bishopsbourne, near Canterbury, and of extensive estates in other parts of Kent. Foote was also vicar of Egerton, on the edge of the Weald, and of other parishes. The *Dictionary of National Biography* has kindly bestowed on him, additionally, the rectory of Bishopsbourne. He made several communications to Hasted about his properties and family history. His son, Sir Edward James Foote (1767–1833), had an adventurous and distinguished career in the navy. An associate of Nelson and favourite of King George III he slightly tarnished his reputation by posthumous attacks on Nelson's memory in connection with certain political events at Naples in 1799. Hasted says only that he was 'in the royal navy'.

Gipps, George (d. 1800)

M.P. for Canterbury and East Kent landowner. He presented to the living of Ringwould his nephew of the same name, whose son, Sir George Gipps (1791–1847), became governor of New South Wales.

Giraud, Francis Frederick (1726–1811)

Headmaster of Faversham grammar school for over forty years. Giraud had been born in Germany of Waldensian refugee stock. These were a Protestant sect founded hundreds of years before the Reformation, who escaped suppression by taking refuge in remote Alpine valleys. Giraud was educated at Oxford, ordained in the English church and preferred to the living of Preston and the curacy of Oare (both near Faversham). He gave Hasted comprehensive details of his parishes and their tithes and charities.

Godfrey, Richard Bernard (b. 1728)

Engraved many of the plates for the *History,* but is better known for his work on the illustrations of the works of the antiquary Francis Grose. Amongst Hasted's papers are Godfrey's pencil drafts of a plate for Chevening.

Hawkins, Thomas (fl. 1788–98)

Of Nash Court, Boughton-under-Blean. This Roman Catholic family had suffered much, Nash Court being plundered every time there was an anti-Popery scare. Four of Thomas's ancestors had achieved some reputation, two as Jesuits and two as authors.

Hawley, Henry (fl. 1779)

The Hawleys succeeded the Whitworths (*see below*) at Leybourne Grange near Maidstone. After Hasted's time, one of Hawley's descendants, Sir Joseph (1813-75) was doubly famous—as a breeder of a Derby winner, and as the owner of the most valuable library in Kent. When Hasted's copy of Weever's *Sepulchral Monuments* came on the market it was noticed that it bore the Hawley bookplate.

Heron, Sir Richard, Bart. (1726–1805)

Became secretary to the Lord Lieutenant of Ireland where he seems to have done a good job until incapacitated by illness. His brother Thomas was owner of Chilham Castle and both plied Hasted with details of their family history. Thomas was most autocratic in laying down in detail what must appear; he provided a printed pedigree which Hasted accepted for inclusion in the account of Chilham. Thomas's son Robert succeeded to the baronetcy on his uncle's death (Thomas having predeceased him) and was a prominent M.P. for many years.

Jacob, Edward (1710–88)

A surgeon, antiquary and naturalist, who became mayor of Faversham. He wrote on the history and botany of Faversham and district and made communications to the Royal Society about elephant bones found on the Isle of Sheppey. Some of his descendants became famous as generals and administrators in India. He was privileged to see and comment upon the proofs of Hasted's accounts of Sheppey.

Knatchbull, Sir Edward (d. 1789)

The Knatchbull family have lived at Mersham near Ashford since the days of Henry VII. They were prominent in national and local affairs from the Long Parliament to the Reform Act, and in the present generation are linked with the Royal Family in marriage and in shared tragedy. Their ancestral home, Mersham Hatch, now houses the Caldecote Community, but bearing the title of Brabourne the family still live in its neighbourhood. The 18th-century Sir Edward supplied a plate of his house, as well as pedigrees and other family details.

Norris, John (d. 1769)

Lived at Benenden in the Weald. His seat Hemsted has since been converted into the girls school at which Princess Anne was educated. Norris's father, Sir John, a renowned admiral, M.P. and plenipotentiary to the Czar of Russia, had the sobriquet of 'Foul-weather Jack', while his ne'er-do-well son had to sell the ancestral estates to meet his debts. The latter is not unknown to history, however, in consequence of his marriage to the notorious Kitty Fraser; an inspirer of many a solacious lampoon she sat for Sir Joshua Reynolds. Hasted left a list of queries about Benenden in John Norris's hands, but the replies have not been traced.

Oxenden, Sir George (1694–1775)

The way the Oxenden family is treated in the *History* shows how closely this is wedded to matters of property and descent at the expense of both broad historical interest and personal achievements. It was perhaps scarcely to be expected that Hasted should mention that his informant about the Walmerstone estate was a notorious profligate and seducer of his own sister-in-law, but perhaps he might have made more of the earlier Sir George (1620–69) who played a decisive role in founding the military power of the East India Company. With Company personnel he successfully defended their Bombay factory from attack by swarms of native warriors when the royal troops had proved unsuccessful. This resulted in the Crown's handing over its military responsibility to the Company and in Oxenden's becoming commander-in-chief. Yet a cursory mention in a footnote is all that this Oxenden receives. Another Oxenden was a distinguished poet, and yet another Vice-Chancellor of Cambridge University.

Papillon, David (fl. 1788)

The Papillons have lived at Acrise Place near Folkestone since 1666. In Hasted's time they had estates widely scattered in the eastern part of Kent, about one of which he sought information. The descent of the family is as illustrious as it is puzzling. The *Dictionary of National Biography* clearly describes how, in 1588, David Papillon, aged seven, and of Huguenot parentage, was brought to England, became a famous military engineer and in 1646 fortified Gloucester for the Parliament. His son was even more prominent as a city merchant and politician, representing Dover at Westminster. When we turn to Hasted's account we find that he has fitted the Papillons up with 'very probable' Norman ancestors. One wonders whether these earlier Papillons returned to France and came over a second time.

Parsons, Philip (1729-1812)

We meet him as the master of Wye School, writing to the printer Bristow to challenge the correctness of the list of curates of Wye given in the *History*. He also supplied news items which were used in the second edition. Rector of Eastwell and Snave, he had before coming to Kent been master of Oakham School, Rutland. He was a 'miscellaneous writer'—how miscellaneous can be judged by the contrast between *Letters to a Friend on the Establishment of a Sunday School* and the anonymously published *Newmarket, or an Essay on the Turf.*

Pegge, Samuel (1704-96)

Gave some help with the accounts of Sundridge and Godmersham (at opposite ends of the county) where he had been respectively curate and vicar. LL.D. and F.S.A. he was interested in antiquities both as a collector and as a prolific writer. After many years in Kent he transferred to a rectory at Whittington, near Chesterfield. His son of the same name was a poet and musical composer as well as an antiquary, while his grandson, Sir Christopher Pegge, was F.R.C.S., F.R.S. and Regius Professor of Physic at Oxford.

Radnor, Lord (1750-1828)

Hasted's patron was the second earl, a Fellow of the Society of Antiquaries. Better known was the third earl (William Pleydell-Bouverie). A Whig politician, he met Marie Antoinette and witnessed the crimes of the French Revolution without being shaken in his radical convictions. He was reputedly the only man with whom William Cobbett never quarrelled; his name has been linked with that of Mary Anne Clarke, ex-mistress of the Duke of York, and great-grandmother of Dame Daphne Du Maurier! His son, another Whig politician, ended by falling out with Gladstone and retiring to his ancestral acres.

Romney, Lord (1712-93)

The family name of the Romneys, seated at Maidstone, was Marsham and an ancestor, Sir John (1612-85), had made a name for himself for his mastery of history, chronology and languages. It was for many years the tradition that the son and heir of the house served Maidstone in Parliament. As early as 1764 the current Lord Romney was telling Hasted that his 'former account' had omitted some item of family history. The family home of the Romneys, the Mote, is now used as a Cheshire Home, providing a link between the 18th century and World War II.

Scott, Edward (fl. 1787)

A descendant of the well-known family of Scott of Scotts' Hall, Smeeth, near Ashford, whose origins are obscured by fabulous claims of royal descent (Scottish). It is the family rather than any single member which figures in the *Dictionary of National Biography*. What seems certain is that they had lived at Scotts' Hall for over three hundred years but sold it shortly before Hasted's account was written, Perhaps their most distinguished member was Reginald (1538-99) who wrote a book attacking witch-hunting, which had influence not only here but also on the Continent. So great was the amount of information, true or false, received by Hasted from Edward Scott that it required footnotes *to* footnotes to accommodate it.

Smythe, Sir Sidney Stafford, Chief Baron of the Exchequer (1705-78)

Was descended from Thomas Smith of Westenhanger near Folkestone, known as 'Customer Smith' from his having farmed the customs of London. Apart from his notorious ill-health when a judge (which drew a sarcastic comment from Lord Mansfield) Smythe is principally remembered for having presided at the sensational trial of Mary Blandy, who was hanged for the murder by arsenic of her own father. It is something of a coincidence that his ancestor 'The Customer' built Corsham Court in the Wiltshire town where Hasted was to end his days. The information of Sir Sidney was entirely about his own family.

Townshend, the Hon. Thomas (1701-80)

Worth mentioning only as being the half-brother of the Chancellor of the Exchequer (Charles) whose taxes lost us our American colonies. Thomas gave Hasted some details about the family seat and manors at Chislehurst.

Twisden, Sir Roger (d. 1772)

The great Kent family of Twysden had two branches, one at Roydon Hall, East Peckham, and the other at Bradbourne, East Malling. To avoid confusion, presumably, the latter branch decided to change the 'y' to an 'i'. The first 'Twisden' was the great judge, Sir Thomas (1612-83). Before his time the Twysdens had included Sir William (1566-1629), gentleman usher to James I and a ripe scholar; John (1607-88), a learned medical writer; and, greatest of all, Sir Roger (1597-1672), a constitutional hero of the Long and Short Parliaments and the Kentish petition. King or Parliament he equally opposed if they tried to act illegally. The incumbent of Bradbourne in Hasted's day was Sir Roger, whose son of the same name provided details about the family and their properties, manors and courts.

Warner, Henry Lee (fl. 1795)

Owner of the Dane John, or Dungeon, manor in Canterbury. The family, later the Lee-Warners, were associated with Walsingham Abbey, Norfolk. They are descended on one side from John Warner (1581–1666), Bishop of Rochester and a devoted adherent of Charles I, and on the other from the Lees, a prominent Canterbury family, one of whom, Henry, was the mayor whom James II unconstitutionally ejected from office, and who also represented the city in Parliament.

Whitworth, Sir Charles (1714–78)

Writer of many books which 'though useful in their day have long been superseded'. He told Hasted the anecdotes of his family 'are already drawn up by Mr. Horace Walpole'. He was perhaps thinking particularly of the experiences in Moscow of his uncle, Charles Baron Whitworth, the diplomat. The Empress Catherine I of Russia greeted him as an old friend and after dancing a minuet squeezed his hand and whispered in his ear 'Have you forgot little Kate?' What happened after that neither history, nor even Horace Walpole relates.

Chapter Six

THE COMMONPLACE BOOKS

IT WAS IMPOSSIBLE to go very far with the job of examining the three great albums of notes or commonplace books without a growing feeling of reluctance bordering almost on distaste and of disenchantment verging on repugnance, for there appeared to be, under each heading, a jumble of jottings lacking all symmetry and excruciatingly difficult to interpret. At the same time there was no prospect of any social interest such as that afforded by the correspondents' letters. However, as time went on certain patterns began to appear; a picture of Hasted at work began to be dimly apparent and a series of interesting discoveries relieved the tedium. These patterns and this picture we can explore, leaving the tedious material in its box in the cathedral strongroom.

Of the three volumes, one is obviously more important and significant than the others. It is the earliest in date and the most comprehensive as regards subject matter. The second, though more voluminous, is merely a continuation of the topographical section of the first, while the third volume records events happening *after* the publication of the *History* and can have no bearing on its composition. The first is indeed the primary volume and for present purposes can be concentrated upon alone.

The arrangement of this compilation is closely wedded, as one would expect, to that of the *History*. First come headed sections corresponding to the topics found in the introductory passages of the *History*, dealing with Kent as a whole. After them, in alphabetical order of place-names, are the notes on the individual parishes and towns with which the bulk of the book is concerned.

Most of the entries record references to the particular place found in Hasted's reading of his books; they cite the pages where the references occur, and usually indicate the subject matter quite briefly. Only occasionally is a lengthy account inserted and this usually happens when there is no book or document to refer back to, as in the case of the much-venerated relic known as the Dumb Borsholder of Chart. This was the name given to a wooden staff about three feet long with sundry iron rings attached and ending in a square spike, which was regarded as a kind of inanimate parish constable. Writes Hasted: 'This Dumb Borsholder was always first called at the Court Leet holden for the Hundred of Twyford; when its keeper, who was yearly appointed by that court held it up to his call, with a neckcloth or handkerchief put through the iron ring fixed at the top, and answered for it'. The keeper collected the annual tribute of one penny which the borsholder claimed from each of 15 houses in the precinct of Pizein-well in the parish of Wateringbury, near Maidstone.

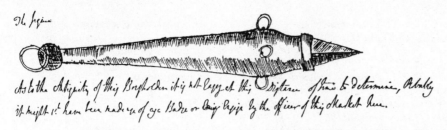

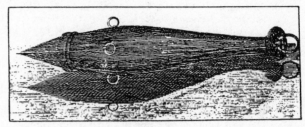

Fig. 7. A sketch of the 'Dumb Borsholder of Chart' from one of Hasted's
commonplace books.

Fig. 8. The much more finished version
of Fig. 7 which the engraver worked up
from Hasted's sketch.

In the Folio, but not in the second edition, there is an engraving of the Dumb
Borsholder. This is based on a sketch of it by Hasted inserted with his account on
a loose sheet in one of the commonplace books. In Wateringbury church they still
treasure the Dumb Borsholder of Chart and it was kept fastened to the wall above
the entrance door. It was removed when vandalistic raids on churches became
frequent, to safer keeping under lock and key. The object thus jealously guarded
has, however, little resemblance to the one depicted in Hasted's sketch and the
engraving based on it.

In the last ninety or so pages there is a reversion to special topics. With whimsical
inconsequence Hasted ends a list of weighty matters with a page of practical hints:
how to get rid of rats, caterpillars and other pests; how to treat stained glass, to
cure chapped lips, to take casts of seals and to make blacking for shoes. Inserted at
the front of the first 'topics' section are two most interesting and revealing items,
a very short list of 'Books in my study to be particularly referred to' and a long
schedule of standard historical works under the heading 'Books which I have not'.

After I had been studying these albums for some time it occurred to me to find
out whether any of the books on Hasted's list were in Canterbury cathedral library;
the answer was an immediate and strong affirmative. All the volumes in the following catalogue are in the Canterbury cathedral library today; all the copies date
from before the writing of Hasted's list, and all appear on it:

    Brady *History of England*, 2 vols. folio, 1687-1700.
    Brady *Treatise on Cities and Boroughs*, 1690.
    Clarendon *History of the Rebellion*, 3 vols. folio, Oxford, 1702-4.
    *Dugdale *Baronage*, 3 vols. folio, 1675-6.
    *Dugdale *History of Embanking*, 1666.
    *Dugdale *Origines Juridiciales*, 1666. (History of English Law and Courts.)
    Fuller *Worthies of England*, 1662.
    Godwin *de Praesulibus*, London, 1620-1627. (Church history.)
    Hickes *Thesaurus*, Oxford, 1703-5, folio. A stupendous book about Anglo-Saxon,
        Icelandic and other northern languages.

*Leland *Collectanea*, 5 vols. Miscellaneous notes on antiquities and catalogues of ancient MSS. (for Leland, *see* p. 136).

*Madox *Exchequer*, 1711. History of the Exchequer from the Conquest to the reign of Edward II.

*Madox *Formulare Anglicanum*. Collection of charters and instruments.

*Plot *Natural History of Oxfordshire*, 1676.

Prynne *Collection of Records* (in the Tower of London), 1689, folio.

*Rushworth *Historical Collections* (17th-century history), 8 vols., 1659–1701.

*Rymer *Foedera*. Public conventions of Great Britain with other powers, authorised by the government of William III, 16 vols., 1704–1713.

*Sandford *Genealogical History* of the monarchs of England 1066–1677, illustrating arms, inscriptions, seals, etc., London, 1677, folio.

Somner *Gavelkind*.

Staveley *History* of churches in England, 1712.

Strype *Ecclesiastical Memorials*, 3 vols. folio, 1721.

*Tanner *Monasticon* (strictly *Notitia Monastica*). History of the religious houses in England and Wales, Oxford, 1695.

*Twysden *Decem Scriptores*. Ten writers of English history, London, 1652 (in Latin). The writers were Simeon of Durham, John of Hexham, Richard of Hexham, Ailred (Ethelred) of Rievaulx, Ralph Deceto, Dean of St Paul's, John Brompton of Jorvaux, Gervase of Canterbury (Cathedral), Thomas Stubbs, William Thorn (St Augustine's) and Henry Knighton.

Wake (Archbishop William) *State of the Church*, 1703, folio.

Wharton *Anglia Sacra*. Lives of archbishops and bishops, 2 vols. folio, London, 1691.

*Wood *Athenae*, 1691-2. Biographies of writers and bishops educated at Oxford, 1500-1690.

*Books marked with an asterisk also appear on Hasted's list of abbreviations (*see* below).

Other 'Books which I have not' include eight or nine works, similar to those set out above, but not to be found in the Canterbury cathedral library today, as well as histories of sundry counties other than Kent, and miscellaneous books and pamphlets, dealing with almost any subject from naval history to fossils.

At the end of this commonplace book there is a prime specimen of that most aggravating of all written productions, a non-alphabetical reference list. Its purpose is to explain the abbreviations used for the titles of the works mentioned in the commonplace books. Some only of the 'Books which I have not' appear in this list of abbreviations (these are starred in the catalogue above). The rest were, one assumes, not read, or if read, produced nothing worth noting. Conversely, the list of abbreviations contains many works not listed either as 'Books in my study' or 'Books which I have not', and to many of these the adjective 'recondite' would not be inappropriate. Take for example the four quarto volumes of the works of Conyers Middleton, a polemical academic and divine, who, so far as is known, never wrote a syllable about the history of Kent or, indeed, any other history later than the time of Cicero; or *Gerrard's Herbal* by Johnson, or Allan on *Waters*, 'being a natural history of chalybeate and purging waters throughout England'. The extent and variety of Hasted's reading is truly amazing. The list of abbreviations shows also that Hasted's notes are not confined to printed books (as he suggested in his letter to Boteler in 1800) but also record points from the collections of manuscripts which he borrowed from his friends, including the Bretts of Wye, Dr. Jacob of Faversham and Charles Whitworth.

In the notes concerning the individual places and parishes, a book described as *Magna Britannia* (an English up-dated version of Camden published in 1769) seems to be specially favoured, in that quite lengthy passages from it are frequently reproduced or perhaps summarised, and moreover these passages occur very early on in the respective notes, sometimes being the first item and sometimes second only to a brief reference to the Warburton manuscript borrowed from Dr. Jacob. This is very significant when one considers the date of *Magna Britannia.* On good archaeological principles one must assume that the extracts from this book *and any subsequent extracts* in the same series of notes cannot have been made earlier than 1769, and that in all probability many of them were, in fact, made much later. As, in fact, most of the notes come after the *Magna Britannia* extracts, then most of the notes were made after 1769. Hasted was therefore embarking, in that year of grace, on a vast course of reading, more appropriate for a scholar preparing to start a book than for one who had already expressed himself as being within reasonable distance of finishing one.[1] What could have happened to cause this apparent change of plan? What was the purpose of the research represented by the commonplace books?

On reflection one is overcome by a certain sense of unreality. In spite of the huge effort that it represents, this research is by no means the primary source of the main narratives of the *History.* A great deal of it resulted only in the insertion, here and there, of odd paragraphs into accounts derived from other sources, and sometimes mere footnotes.[2] Linked with this significant circumstance is another, namely the absence of any reference in the commonplace books to four sources which Hasted used copiously (as shown by his own acknowledgements in footnotes and by comparisons of texts). These are: The Escheat Rolls; Lambarde's *Perambulation*; Philipott's *Villare Cantianum*; and Harris's *History of Kent.*

These four sources require a word of explanation. The expression 'escheat rolls' is used by Hasted, and the writers whose works he copied, to mean the records of the *post mortem* inquisitions, or enquiries, which formed part of the machinery of the feudal system. An important object of these inquisitions was to ascertain who was entitled to succeed to the estates of the deceased; only if he left no heir did the lands *escheat* to the king. The recorded results enabled the Exchequer to claim what was due to the Crown and (perhaps equally importantly) provided the genealogists with the materials for family histories. It is not to be supposed that Hasted regularly, or indeed ever, referred to the originals of these records; one suspected that he used, rather, other men's calendars and extracts, or references found in the books he was copying. (For a further discussion of this point *see* Appendix III.)

The other three sources are printed books. Lambarde's *Perambulation,* the first of all county histories, was published in the reign of Elizabeth I and reflects the Protestant predelictions of that reign. Much space is taken up with denunciations of Popery and superstition, and a few more solid facts would have been acceptable. Thomas Philipott's *Villare Cantianum,* a survey of Kent in alphabetical order, dealing mainly with the estates of the landed gentry, was a 17th-century production considered to be full of blunders and guesswork. The *History of Kent* by John Harris, who died in 1719, is described in the *Dictionary of National Biography* as 'of little value' and 'extremely inaccurate'. These, then, were the works that Hasted used and followed extensively. With the help of these sources he was able to carry his story of the descents of the manors and the genealogy of their owners down to about 1660, at which point his fountains of information dried up because the inquisitions *post mortem* and many other feudal survivals were then abolished. Lambarde was obviously no longer any help. Philipott ended his account in 1656, and Harris did little more than reproduce Philipott. The three

Fig. 9.   The Dark Entry, in the precincts of Canterbury Cathedral, as it was in Victorian times. The tall house on the right, of which only a corner can be seen, is thought to have been Hasted's Canterbury home. The house was demolished many years ago.

printed sources were therefore deficient in two respects: first, they were in varying degrees incomplete, inadequate or unreliable; and, secondly, they did not cover the last century before the time when Hasted started on his *History*. The latter deficiency was only to a slight degree covered by Warburton's survey of 1725, and Hasted had to rely on enquiries of landowners, attorneys and other knowledgeable persons to complete his information; this is proved by the questionnaires found in the correspondence.

Conjecture is dangerous, and liable to add to the store of Hasted legends, but it seems reasonably safe to assert on the known facts that sometime about the year 1770 a great change of heart occurred, leading Hasted to feel dissatisfied with the work he had already done, and the methods and sources he had been using. He therefore embarked on a wider course of study. But why pick on the Canterbury cathedral library for his purpose? London would perhaps involve more expense, but Rochester would be as cheap, and nearer to St John's. The answer may be that Hasted wanted also to work in the Prerogative Office of Canterbury (where the wills were kept). Perhaps he was by now beginning to feel the financial draught, so that a move to Canterbury would kill three birds with one stone--the cathedral library would provide the books, the Prerogative Office the wills, and the cathedral precincts a more economical way of life. For whatever reason, it was to Canterbury that Hasted came, and the first three volumes of his *History* were completed there, before more dramatic events transferred the scene of action to some very strange places indeed.

Chapter Seven

THE MAIDSTONE COLLECTION

ONCE IT BECAME EVIDENT that the Irby papers were a possible key to the whole mystery of Hasted's methods and sources, it went without saying that the investigation could not end with the filing of my report on the Canterbury materials; it must be pursued anywhere and everywhere that Hasted documents were to be found. Professor Everitt's Introduction to the reprint of the second edition had revealed, for the uninitiated, the whereabouts of a good deal of this material—in the British Museum (now Library) there should be sixty or seventy books and volumes of manuscripts; in the Maidstone Museum (in addition to Hasted's letters to Thomas Astle and his *Anecdotes of the Hasted family,* both already published) notebooks and more documents; and lastly, in the Rochester Museum, 'a mass of legal documents' concerning Hasted's financial difficulties and the loss and recovery of his ancestral estates. Rochester could be put aside for the moment, since its contribution would be connected with Hasted's private life rather than with the writing of the *History,* and between Maidstone and the British Library the former seemed the easier to start on.

The general impression received from reading the Irby papers was that they related predominantly to the later period of the writing of the *History,* from about 1770 onward, when Hasted had (one assumed) become dissatisfied with his earlier work, and had moved to Canterbury to collect information from the cathedral library and the probate records. In 'Irby' relatively little attention is given to family pedigrees, still less to heraldry, although these were two of the historian's greatest preoccupations, and the papers do not impinge very markedly on the more ancient period of the property descents. One would therefore hope to find in the British Library, if not also at Maidstone, the raw materials for Hasted's writings on these topics, and perhaps the solution to the mystery of the Roman numerals.

The Hasted papers at the Maidstone [Municipal] Museum were under the immediate care of David Kelly, who, in addition to his local government post, holds that of Honorary Curator of the collections of the Kent Archaeological Society, both museums being housed in Chillington Manor House, an ancient building which has survived in the heart of commercial Maidstone.

After such a long mental entanglement with the one single mass of documents at the cathedral library, it was a refreshing change to tackle another collection. Hasted's *Anecdotes* and letters to Astle (which David Kelly courteously produced) with the so-familiar handwriting, though no surprise, gave me a certain feeling of quasi-proprietorship. Less expected was the casual production of the greater part of the manuscript of F IV of which there had been no previous warning. On the other hand, four vellum-bound notebooks likewise laid before me had been mentioned by Professor Everitt. Other complete surprises were a letter from Hasted to Sir Joseph Banks and a bond of the historian for securing the repayment of the sum of £550 with interest to one Richard Gibbs.[1]

The manuscript of the Folio volume was a fair copy to the extent that there were no alterations or interlineations visible, although here and there a new version had been pasted over an older one. Occasionally a gap was left in the narrative with pencilled dimensions and an instruction to the printer to leave the space for an engraving. This explained how Hasted could be involved in to-ings and fro-ings with Boteler about engravings even after the copy had gone to the printer. It was only a year or two later, after the manuscript had been transferred to the county archives that, looking at it again, I found that the printer, Simmons, had had to modernise several of Hasted's old-fashioned spellings. The manuscript had 'lyes' for 'lies', 'beautifull', 'murthered' for 'murdered', 'intervalls', 'Doomsday' as well as the modern version of 'Domesday', and 'seized' (in the legal sense of possessed) for 'seised'. There was also a profuse employment of capitals for common nouns and adjectives which Simmons had corrected. A writer so behind the times in orthography seemed less likely (I thought) than ever to have been responsible for the modernistic tone of some of the additions made in the second edition.

Hasted's letter to Sir Joseph can speak for itself. Banks' reply (p. 51) is dated the very next day, even though travel was by horse-power and Canterbury and London fifty or sixty miles apart:

> Sir,
>   I am sorry again to trouble you for your assistance towards my History of this County, but being now come to print my account of the parish of Norton, and of Provenders in it, I could wish to mention something of your descent and arms, the same as I do of other gentlemen of the County; the connexion has been of so small a space of time, that I am not at present enabled to give more than the name of yourself, which is so far short of every other that I hope you will favor me with so much as will render my account equal at least to the rest of my work, and thereby make it satisfactory to the public and I hope not unpleasing to yourself. My mention sir of yourself too, and the voyages you have undertaken, the object and result of them, may not perhaps be so satisfactory to you as I could wish; therefore I hope to receive the favor of such instructions as you think best, to enable me to mention them with truth and to your own liking, which will be esteemed an obligation conferred on him who is with much respect sir
>
>   Your most obedient servant
> Canterbury   EDWARD HASTED.
> July 25th 1672

The first of the four vellum-bound notebooks contains such a bewildering assortment of items that it is difficult to improve on Hasted's title for it: *Collect. Varia and C. Kent Respect.* (Various collections connected with the county of Kent.) It is undated but the spine is endorsed with, in addition to the title, Roman numerals undecipherable owing to wear and tear. After pages of extracts from parish registers, all in Hasted's hand (as are the contents of all four of the books), there is a note of a decree in Chancery and pages of copy of a legal document all relating to Joiner's charity at Stowting which, typically, is not mentioned in the *History* at all. After more lengthy parochial extracts we have excerpts from Spelman's *Glossary* (of legal terms), lists of Admirals, Chancellors and Constables of England; notes on the Anglo-Saxon pound, and 'Danegeld or Hydrage'. The rest consists of notes about Dugdale's *Monasticon,* giving the pages at which different topics are dealt with. Hasted, as we recall, had told Astle that he intended to go through this book extracting matters relating to Kent.

The second notebook, again with half-effaced Roman numerals on the spine, is entirely written in Latin. In the first part, Hasted copies extracts made by Sir Edward Dering of Surrenden 'from a very large and very old register' relating to Canterbury Cathedral. It consists, in effect, of copies of copies. References to shrines and altars precede calendars of numbered 'charters', i.e., legal deeds granting privileges and so forth to the monks. Some of the benefactors are kings of England and of France, and William the Conqueror contributes the Accord of Winchester concerning the subjection of the see of York to that of Canterbury. Always a favourite subject matter for legal documents are 'compositions' that the monks entered into with other parties, sorting out legal wrangles, and many of these are listed. Richard de Clare, Earl of Gloucester, appears as a benefactor of the monastery, and perhaps it is in view of his interests in Tonbridge that a perambulation of the Lowy (surrounding district) of Tonbridge is included. There are copies of documents concerning various parishes of the city of Canterbury and the different altars in the cathedral (important sources of revenue from pious offerings), and a list of charters 'de Anniversariis'. Ecclesiastical historians may explain the significance of these entries. This part ends with a list of the manors and properties belonging to the monks.

Hasted then begins the copying of another book of transcripts, starting with the title page. It bears the date 1630, which suggests that this may be another product of the industry of Sir Edward Dering, although his name is not mentioned. These extracts are a baffling mixture; in the first part communications from various popes are mixed with a calendar of yet more charters relating to Canterbury Cathedral, varied in the later part by records of court proceedings against clergy.

The third notebook again has the title and a Roman numeral reference written on the spine, rendered only half-legible by age and use. The book consists of extracts from the cartularies of Horton Priory and Bayham Abbey, and against five of the items Hasted has written 'See T. XC page —' different page numbers being quoted. The extracts are stated to have been made by or on the orders of Sir Edward Dering in 1627. Between the calendars of the charters of the two monasteries are sandwiched other lengthy items including a rental, a terrier, and a list of the churches in the Canterbury diocese not appropriated to ecclesiastical bodies, and one of those that were so appropriated.

The last notebook is stated to be transcribed by Hasted from copies of entries in the registry of St Augustine's monastery made in 1628 and possessed by Sir Robert Cotton, Bart.[2] The extracts seem to be copied from three separate manuscripts of which the contents can be summarised as follows:

(1) a list of dated historical events beginning with the advent of Hengist
    and Horsa, the rule of Vortigern, and other happendings in A.D. 449,
    followed by the dates of the reigns of English kings down to Henry III,
    and of the enthronements of the archbishops down to the same epoch;
    an account of the rule of St Benedict, and of the privileges of St
    Augustine's Abbey; more charters.
(2) Dated 1629; as varied as (1), the items distinguished as numbered
    chapters, and relating to religious events such as the instalment of an
    abbot or the occurrence of a miracle, and to property grants.
(3) Undated, but commences with a copy of the 'Blake Booke' of the
    treasury of St Augustine, 1392, being a calendar of charters relating
    to the property of the monastery and the giving of homage by its
    tenants.

Hasted's notes then revert to the English language with the title 'Extracts from
a register of St Augustine's, 1392, the great rental of all the manors and other
lands of the said monastery in the time of Thomas Fyndon, Abbat'. The list of
monkish lands ends with this note: 'See more of this Register P. LXXXI Vol. 5
p, 120'. Another mystery to solve!

The many hundreds of pages of neatly written notes to be found in these four
books remind one overwhelmingly of the enormous time and effort that Hasted
devoted to copying. This kind of material can best be compared with an immense
volume of ore from which is yielded a tiny proportion of metal. Obviously the
historian had no particular points in mind on which he needed information when
making these copies. He began as a collector of manuscripts and ended as the
historian of Kent; this copying of other men's extracts represents, it would seem,
an intermediate stage in this transformation. The writing, though obviously from
the same hand that wrote the correspondence with Boteler and the MS. of the
fourth Folio volume is that of a less sophisticated person, and one in less of a
hurry; it is more rounded and perfect and carefully executed, and seems to flow
uniformly forward like the work of a professional scribe.

Before leaving the Maidstone Museum I made the unexpected discovery that there
were on the premises copies of the antiquarian magazine *Bibliotheca Topographica
Britannica*, the first issue of which had contained, according to John Thorpe, an
attack on the first volume of Hasted's *History*. The Museum, in fact, possessed that
very number. The criticism of Hasted comes in the final paragraph of the Preface to
an account of the antiquities of the village of Tunstall, near Sittingbourne, and
comes presumably from the hand of the great John Nichols, the publisher of
the series:

> So much may suffice for the original design of this little history. In its
> execution Mr. Mores may be fairly presumed to have exerted all that the
> *dulcedo natalis foli* [sweetness of one's native soil] calls forth. He professes
> to have drawn his materials chiefly from printed books. Had the compiler
> of the general history of that county, of which Tunstall makes so small a
> part, confined himself only to those sources, how much would he have
> improved that long-expected and voluminous work! But had he penetrated
> more intimately (for notwithstanding the profession of the preface, scarce

any such appear among his authorities) into the $\kappa\epsilon\iota\mu\eta\lambda\iota\alpha$ [treasures] of records, inquisitions, chartularies, registers, and that fund of materials which are open to every diligent investigator, what a history of KENT, that county of Britain to which her first invader pays such a compliment, would have arisen under the pen of Mr. Hasted!

Returning to Canterbury with this important information, I was informed that there was a history of Tunstall in the cathedral library. After some searching I found the volume which was inscribed with the title *Antiquities of Tunstall,* but proved to be merely a bound copy of the first issue of *Bibliotheca Topographica Britannica.* The criticism of Hasted has been under my nose all the time.

Having dealt with the minor literary outwork of Maidstone, the humble investigator was now emboldened to attack the main fortress of learning itself, the British Museum, or British Library as the section devoted to books and manuscripts must now be called.

Chapter Eight

THE BRITISH LIBRARY

MY PRELIMINARY LETTER to the Keeper of Manuscripts at the British Library fired off a number of pertinent queries about two mysteries: the assertion in that old handbook that Hasted's MSS. in the library had been purchased in 1770, eight years before the appearance of the first volume of the *History*; and the Roman numerals puzzle.

By great good fortune, the research assistant to whom my letter was referred turned out to be the son of a neighbour of mine so that the ice was broken at once, and one of the problems quickly cleared up; the MSS., from indications in the manuscript catalogue of the Library, were purchased in 1795 or thereabouts, not 1770. The Roman numerals, however, were not immediately explained, as all Hasted's MSS. had been labelled with Additional MSS. numbers in Arabic and not Roman figures. Any idea that the MSS. would be similar to the notebooks seen at Maidstone received a quick negative when my friendly informant (Peter Jones) reported that the MSS. seemed to have been bound by the British Museum, and were of various sizes. However, further research by Peter brought yet more interesting information, still in advance of any visit to the Library. He sent me a copy of the entry in the manuscript catalogue for Additional MSS. 5536 and 5537, which were almost certainly the two quarto index volumes mentioned by Hasted in his letter to Boteler of 24 March 1800:

> At the end of the first volume pp. 261–277 is a list of the whole of Mr. Hasted's MSS. with the marks by which they were distinguished and referred to, and at the end of the second volume pp. 305–331 another copy of the same list, enlarged with indications in pencil of those MSS. not bought with the rest of his collection for the Museum; the Trustees having (perhaps injudiciously) declined to purchase what were merely Mr. Hasted's own collectanea and compilations.

To quote from Peter Jones's further letter:

> . . . the two lists of MSS. mentioned give the Roman numeration used by Hasted for all his manuscripts, including those *not* bought by the B.M. Each number is preceded by a letter which was perhaps originally a shelf-mark. Thus the first is A.I and the last Z.CIX (or Z.CXIII in the other list, which is not identical).

I next supplied Peter with as much as could be deciphered of the inscriptions on the spines of the Maidstone notebooks (Roman numerals and written titles), with the result that three of the four were provisionally identified with entries on Hasted's list of his MSS. And the T XC references (see p. 84) corresponded to pages in Add. MS. 5516 that related to Horton Priory, which was, in fact, registered by Hasted as T. XC.

After these useful preliminaries, my first visit to the British Library was on 10 August 1978, and I thus described it in a letter to a valued friend, the Rev. S. G. Brade-Birks, formerly vicar of Godmersham, near Canterbury, but now, alas!, no longer with us:

> I had heard that it was a terrible job studying documents there; I had been warned of the difficulty of getting a seat in competition with swarms of Commonwealth students turned out of their lodgings by their land-ladies, and of the hours of delay waiting for the requested MS. to appear, but my experience was quite different. The only delay was in getting enrolled, which is due to the tight security. My credentials were scrutin-ised, and I was photographed in colour, then issued with a ticket. Then I went into the students' reading room—quite a small one—and chose a place; there were plenty available. Next I obtained a supply of the forms you have to fill for each document required (up to three at a time). The completed forms are put through a sort of letter box into the next room, and you return to your seat to await delivery. I had scarcely got back to my place before the three MSS. were handed to me. I had, of course, given warning by letter of which ones I wanted to see.
>
> The three documents I chose were first the one designated by Hasted as T XC, and referred to in a notebook in the Maidstone Museum trans-cribed by Hasted and concerned with Horton Priory. The MS. was a little book with copies of charters written in a medieval hand stuck in. The Maidstone references tallied with it entirely, e.g., when Maidstone said 'Henry of Essex grants alms' followed by a reference, the corresponding section of the BL document began (from memory) *Sciant omnes fideles presentes et futuri quod ego Henricus de Essesia* (&c.).
>
> Second and third I had picked nos. 5536 and 5537, 'General index to his MSS. relating to the county of Kent 1769'. These proved to be more like commonplace books than indices, but at the end of each was a real index, namely a list in numerical order of the MSS. according to Hasted's code of letters followed by Roman figures. This is what I have long been looking for, as references in this code appear frequently in the Irby deposit documents that I have been studying . . .
>
> They also have at the BL a MS. catalogue giving a description of each document, and I went through this, to find that the great bulk of the material acquired from Hasted does not bear on his history. Indeed, my impression so far is that only about a dozen of the sixty-odd MSS. bought from Hasted will really interest me. This is wonderful, as it means that this preliminary visit has reduced my supposed task to about a fifth of what I had anticipated. I need not concern myself with preparations for the conquest of Ireland, the reorganisation of the navy, or sequestrations of benefices in East Anglia.

On one of the two versions of Hasted's list of his own manuscripts, someone had written, in miniscule pencil figures against each relevant item, the number assigned to it in the Additional MSS.—an invaluable aid.

After many visits to the Library, and careful study of the lengthy entries in the manuscript index, and, where the effort seemed to be worthwhile and necessary, the MSS. themselves, it was possible to assess the results as follows:

> There are 122 MSS. on Hasted's list, of which 59 are not in the British Library, they being obviously the ones that the trustees 'injudiciously' decided not to purchase. Of the sixty-odd MSS. that *are* in the Library, well over half either do not relate to Kent at all, or relate to it only in common with other parts of the country: All are summarised in the British Library's MS. catalogue, and perhaps some indication would be expected here as to what the non-Kent MSS. are about. However, with the best will in the world it is impossible *briefly* to describe them. For instance, Add. 5482 begins with lists of Knights of the Garter in the time of Elizabeth I (collected by Robert Knight) and ends with receipts for the cure of earache. Even disregarding the household hints, one finds the documents too varied to classify: Add. 5489 (from A. Hill's collection) is about the dissection of dead bodies, trade with Smyrna, a Cornish rebellion, voyages in Italy and Germany, the plague at Amsterdam, and Newfoundland fisheries; and, I hesitate to add, more medical prescriptions. The organisation of the navy and preparations to invade Ireland are topics found in other MSS. There seems to be one group with a common denominator—sequestrations of benefices during the Commonwealth.

The words 'From A. Hill's collection' are more significant when it is discovered that Abraham Hill was a well-known man of science, and a founder member of the Royal Society (*see* p. 123). The identification is certain, since Hill ended his days at Sutton-at-Hone and owned St John's, the house where Hasted later resided; and after Hill's death some at least of his papers are supposed to have passed into the hands of Thomas Astle.

Add. 5488 is, on Hasted's list, F. XIX 'Familiar Letters to Abm Hill, Esqr. from different persons'. The surprising fact is that Thomas Astle is stated to have published a selection of the correspondence of Abraham Hill under almost the same title and one wondered whether Astle was introduced to the letters by Hasted. A close study of Add. 5488 and the text of the book in the British Library showed, quite amazingly, that the credit for the book should have gone to Hasted rather than Astle (*see* Chapter Thirteen),

Equally productive of mystery is Add. 5485 (E. XV on Hasted's list) 'A book containing sundry matters and records of various kinds respecting different counties'. Here we meet a great array of antiquarian talent. The items come chiefly from the collections of Sir H. St George, Clarenceux, and belonged to John Anstis, Garter King of Arms. One item is from the collection of Sir William le Neve, another well-known herald and genealogist, and many of the charters were copied from the collections of Robert Glover, Somerset Herald, 'one of the most accomplished heralds and genealogists that this country has produced'. He came from Ashford, Kent, and is briefly mentioned in Hasted's *History*. However, none of these MSS. seems to be original, but bafflingly some of the transcripts are in the hands of Anstis, whose MSS. are stated to have passed, after his death, into the possession of Thomas Astle. How then did these transcripts come into the ownership of Hasted?

There are indeed precisely 12 documents that are of service to the student of the history of Kent as a whole,[2] but there are others that would be important to anyone interested in specialist subjects or individual institutions. Three volumes are an index, in Hasted's hand, to Harris's *History of Kent*; then there are documents concerning the Dering family of Surrenden and manorial rolls from the area round Sutton-at-Hone. The Horton Priory documents we have already heard about, but can now note that Hasted used them freely in his account of the Priory (F III 318-9). Other material relates to Wye College and Canterbury Cathedral.

The dozen pan-Kentish documents can be divided into four categories. The first consists of copies of records of heraldic visitations made by members of the College of Arms. Their purpose was to check that coats of arms were being correctly used, and to record the pedigrees of those entitled to bear them. Three of the four MSS. in this group are based on the famous visitation in 1619 by John Philipott, Rouge Dragon, who is specially well-known in Kent as the father of Thomas Philipott, the ostensible author of *Villare Cantianum,* the book on whose structure Hasted's *History* is largely founded; it is commonly accepted, moreover, that the book was nearly all written by the father, John, and published by his son without acknowledgement of this fact. The remaining visitation is somewhat earlier, that of Robert Cooke, Clarenceux, in 1574.

The next group consists of family pedigrees. Most of them are ancient collector's pieces or the result of speculative random copying by Hasted. An exception is Add. 5520 (X. CIII on his own list). This book of MSS. containing 121 pedigrees stands out because the items were collected, and many of them actually composed by Hasted himself, specifically for the *History*.

The third category of these more important documents can best be described as 'miscellaneous', yet is perhaps the most interesting, containing as it does many sketches of buildings and scenes.

In a category of its own is Add. MS. 5483 (E. X. on Hasted's list, and in his hand) described as extracts from the ancient Exchequer records. One unfortunate characteristic of this document is that it is mostly in Latin! Hasted's title page says that the extracts are from the 'Originalia, Memoranda, Inquisitions, post mortem and Liberate rolls &c.'. Where had he obtained his information? With no training in the study of ancient archives, and living out of London, so that he would have no opportunity to repair by constant and prolonged study of the records his lack of formal training, Hasted would, one imagines, be quite incapable of making these extracts unaided from the original records.[3] A parallel problem concerning his quotations from the Harleian MSS. suggested a possible solution. The latter documents are frequently cited in the *History* as authorities, and in the Irby collection there were several pages of extracts from or notes about the Harleian MSS., the use of which could be traced in the *History*. It was discovered, however, that in the British Library there was an index of the MSS., the earlier part of which had been made by the librarian Humfrey Wanley in the early part of the 18th century, and that the entries on Hasted's lists were simply copies of those entries in Wanley's index that referred to Kent. The extracts covered only one section of the index (nos. 283 to 6835 inclusive), but it is almost certain that they formed part of document O. LXXI on Hasted's list ('A catalogue of the MSS. in the Harleian collection in the British Museum relating to the County of Kent'), all the rest of which is missing.

Had something similar happened with the Exchequer extracts? Having obtained a reader's pass for the Public Record Office and having sent a preliminary letter outlining the problem, I spent much time searching old and obsolete indexes and calendars to find Hasted's source, but without success. There are, of course, many modern calendars of the Exchequer records, but it was necessary to find ones that existed in Hasted's day, and this proved to be very difficult. It seems that the Exchequer officers themselves, as far back as the 16th century, are known to have compiled volumes of extracts, and that this practice continued in the 17th, 18th and early 19th centuries, the archivists Agarde and le Neve being specially prominent in this type of work. A member of the Record Office staff told me that officers of the courts derived part of their income from searching for, copying, and even translating documents, so that for an inexperienced person research would be expensive rather than impossible. The librarian of the Society of Antiquaries produced a most interesting but little-known book, *Observations on the State of Historical Literature,* by Nicholas Harris Nicolas (1830) which showed that, before the system was reformed in the 19th century, the cost of researching into the original records by those capable of doing it was almost prohibitive. In fine, one suspects that the obliging Thomas Astle may well have put in Hasted's way a number of calendars of the Exchequer records from which the would-be historian could extract the Kentish matter. We should perhaps have had some clues to help elucidate this problem if documents E. XIII on Hasted's list were available, but it is not. It is described as 'Extracts from the Escheat Rolls Knights' fees and the possessors of them, Account of Lands held in Capite, Scutages, Lands held of Dover Castle and the Ward and services due from them. Divers extracts from the Red Book of the Exchequer and other matters comprehended under the title of Feoda Cantiana'.

However that may be, the study of the manuscripts in the British Library had at least shown that the amount of material bearing upon the *History* could be reduced to manageable proportions. But what greater knowledge would have been forthcoming if the trustees had purchased for the British Museum the whole of Hasted's manuscripts.

For a description in greater detail of the 12 more important manuscripts, *see* Appendix I.

Chapter Nine

'MR. CLUDGE'

THE EXAMINATION OF the Irby deposit was now completed, for the time being at any rate. There had indeed been some wanderings from the path, but it was now entirely traversed and the resulting report had been lodged in the cathedral archives. The calendar of the correspondents' letters alone occupied over eighty pages, and the correspondence between William Boteler and Hasted, photocopied, filled an even thicker file. But what might have been supposed to be the end was at the same time a beginning because the tree of research bears more than one type of fruit. There are first the actual tangible results that can be committed to paper and which are no matter for argument but sheer solid fact—the long calendars of letters were of this character, as was the incidental discovery that there were two printed versions of F I—for the calendars can be compared with the original letters and the two versions of the volume can be shown side by side and compared: there can be no dispute.

Research, however, has another less tangible but no less important result when, as a result of prolonged study of the material, familiarity with it gives rise to convictions, or at least theories, based on general impression rather than specific factual data. In this way ideas about the characters of Hasted and his principal informants had already begun to take shape. The historian was emerging as a scissors-and-paste man, energetic at seeking out sources, mainly, as he admitted, in printed books, but making little effort to interpret or make a synthesis of what he found, simply repeating the words of his sources as he found them, with or without acknowledgement; his wit was usually second-hand, and his imagination quite dormant. Having received these impressions I discovered, at first by accident and later after deliberate searching, a number of passages in the *History* which displayed the original qualities that Hasted lacked, and which were, in fact, borrowed from other writers. The first example that I happened to notice was the use without acknowledgement of a mild witticism of William Lambarde. The Perambulator of Kent had referred to the uncertainty about the exact boundaries of the Weald and had concluded that 'as it is now in manner wholly replenished with people, a man may more reasonably maintain that there is no Weald at all, than certainly pronounce either where it beginneth, or maketh an end'. Suitably modernised, this aphorism went straight into Hasted's account as if the thought was his own. An even more flagrant plagiarism is the entertaining account of events at Minster-in-Thanet in the 17th century. It concerns the exploits of one Richard Culmer, a notorious Puritan fanatic, responsible for unspeakable vandalism at Canterbury Cathedral. After mentioning two crosses on the top of the church spire at Minster,

Hasted describes how Culmer (who had got control of the parish by sequestration) 'took it into his fancy that these were monuments of superstition and idolatry' and had them removed. 'But', adds Hasted, 'if all the figures of a cross are monuments of idolatry, and to be removed, the poor caitiff has done his work but by halves, or rather not at all, when he took down these from the spire and left the church standing, which is in itself in the form of a cross.' Well done, Hasted! one is inclined to exclaim until one finds out that, except for one word the whole passage is copied, without acknowledgement, from Lewis's *History of Thanet*. Lewis indeed, instead of 'poor caitiff', had written 'poor man', which I think is better. Hasted also copied from Lewis, without acknowledgement, the account of the Goodwin Sands which William Boys so strongly criticised. Descriptions of the scenery of east Kent, of Caesar's invasion route, and of the intermittently flowing Nailbourne are lifted from a work of Dr. Packe, but this time with acknowledgement.

The discovery that these and other noteworthy passages were borrowed from other people's writings strengthened the impression of Hasted as being without originality or distinction as a writer, but to confirm this opinion I obviously had to seek as many examples as could be traced. Searching for them, I made an even more surprising discovery, one so unexpected that one could scarcely proclaim it for fear of being thought to be quite irresponsible.

The seeds of this heresy were sown at Stelling Minnis, a tract of unenclosed common lying some seven or eight miles south of Canterbury amid some of the quietest and most remote countryside of Kent, between the Elham Valley and Stone Street. Long before I was concerned with the Irby deposit I had noticed Hasted's striking reference to the people who lived on the Minnis: 'The inhabitants . . . are as wild, and in as rough a state as the country they dwell in'. And I was not the only person to notice this passage; in the monograph preceding the reprint of the second edition it is quoted as being one of those 'brief but telling descriptions' which show that Hasted's work was more than a mere history of Kent. In the light of Culmer and the Goodwin Sands it seemed more than probable that this arresting phrase was not Hasted's own but a borrowing. I had noticed these words quite early in my acquaintance with the *History* when I still regarded the second edition as the canon, but I was wiser now and turned to the Folio hoping to read the authentic, undiluted and unabridged original version, and also perhaps some clue in a footnote as to the source of the passage. Then came the shock, the astonishing discovery that the passage is not to be found in the first edition at all!

Before trying to find out why this notable sentence should appear for the first time in the second edition of the *History*, it seemed a good idea to enquire whether this was a unique instance or one of many. I therefore proceeded to test any passage that had caught my attention while reading the second edition. There was, for instance, the remark about Lenham, between Ashford and Maidstone, where the inhabitants greet you with the exclamation: 'Ah, Sir, poor Lenham!'; the semi-blasphemous rhyme about Hever: 'Jesus Christ never was but once at Hever, and then he fell into the river'; and again, the account of the martin cats (like those at Hudson's Bay) at Mereworth; and fourthly, the lyrical description of the river scenery at East Barming near Maidstone.

No sign of any of these memorable passages of the second edition was to be found in the Folio! As a result, a flash of insight prompted me to ask myself whether the second edition was indeed Hasted's unaided work. The only thing to do was to test the hypothesis thoroughly by comparing the accounts of all the six hundred-odd places described in the respective editions.

The results, bearing in mind that Hasted was in prison during the whole of the time that the second edition was being prepared, are quite unbelievable: of 80 parishes described in F I, 56 are virtually described afresh in the second edition; in F II there are 115 parochial descriptions, and 67 of them are substantially altered. There are fewer alterations in F III and F IV, particularly in the remoter regions such as Romney Marsh and the Isle of Sheppey. There are no alterations to the accounts of the Thanet parishes, not really surprising since there was only a matter of months between the publication of the first and second edition accounts of these places.

So there had been wholesale alterations. At first sight this fact alone was suspicious, but suspicion is not proof. Was it possible that Hasted himself had really written the new passages, confined as he was? Did the new material, by its style and vocabulary, give any clue? Was it the sort of stuff that he *might* have written? The only thing to do was to read the rival accounts side by side with close attention for possible leads.

The first topographical article of all is on Deptford and comparison is difficult because of the confusing way in which different paragraphs and even sentences had been switched about in the second edition. It did however emerge that the following paragraph was printed for the first time in the second edition:

> In the lower part of Deptford are the two churches of St Nicholas and St Paul, as is the scite of the ancient mansion of Saye's Court, long since demolished, the present building on it being made use of, as the parish workhouse of St Nicholas, the only remains of its former state being two brick piers of a large gateway. Near it is still remaining the holly hedge mentioned by Evelyn in his *Sylva*.

Now how could Hasted in his prison, and so far as one knows not having visited Deptford for many years, know anything about holly hedges still remaining, more especially as he was not sufficiently interested in Evelyn even to mention his *Sylva*? Evidently Sayes Court must have been converted into a workhouse after the date of the first edition, but how could Hasted have known details such as the two brick piers being left? At the very least he must have had an informant who had made a close inspection.

Repeatedly in his first edition Hasted dismisses the parishes as having 'nothing worthy of notice' while in the second edition the writer usually manages at least half a page of description. Thus the town of Eltham has, in the second edition, more than that amount of new descriptive matter. Indeed, each successive place seems to have a greatly extended and circumstantial description, conjuring up an eye witness impression which it would be quite impossible for a person who had not seen the place for many years to compose unless he had both a photographic memory and a vivid imagination.

Cudham is another place which in the Folio Hasted dismisses as having 'nothing in it worthy of particular notice'. In the Octavo, however, there is the best part of a page of description, referring to people and places not mentioned in the first edition, as well as much topographical detail. There is an even more striking contrast at St Paul's Cray where again Hasted says that the village has nothing 'worthy particular notice in it'. In the second edition there is a whole page of lively description: 'The church stands alone', we read, 'half surrounded by tall elms the shade of which cast a pleasing gloom and makes a picturesque appearance to the building as well as the churchyard round it'. Later there is reference to the parish being 'diversified with hill and dale, interspersed with woods and verdant pastures along the valleys and on the gentle declivities and fertile fields of cornland'.

Erith provides another example of a greatly lengthened description, including the following: '. . . on the east side of the road leading from the heath towards the church is a cottage not improperly so styled, being upon a very small scale indeed, erected by John Maddocks, Esq. late of Vale Mascall, near North Cray, who gave it the name of Holly Hill and resides in it. It is a neat and elegant box and from it there is a delightful view of the Thames and of the county of Essex beyond it'. This surely must be an eye-witness description.

Another touch of local colour is found at Wilmington, near Dartford, where the second edition mentions that 'the quantity of cherry grounds which encircle the village contribute much to the pleasantness of its experience and in the spring when the trees are in blossom it seems a continued range of gardens'. Farningham provides a good example of the familiar style of the rewriting. We learn that the River Darent 'meanders its silver stream across the parish northward in the midst of a valley of fertile meadows. The corn mill is built on a most expensive mechanical construction and there are two capital inns forming altogether a situation remarkably healthy and pleasant and exceedingly convenient for its accommodations in every respect'.

Many of the parishes in west Kent, including Penshurst, receive a page or more of descriptive matter not to be found in the first edition; in this Edenbridge is typical. Hasted (first edition) gives five lines to the description of the village which in the second edition is expanded to a full page, including the following graphic depiction:

> The country here bears a far different aspect from that before described above the hills, the soil being for the most part a deep tillage land of stiff clay, moist and swampy, the hedgerows round the field broad and much filled with broad spreading oaks, and the roads deep and miry, broad, and very much covered with green swerd; the farmhouses are old fashioned timber buildings standing single and much dispersed, all which give the country rather a gloomy appearance, but whatever it may want in pleasantness is made up by the health, fertility of soil, and its many local advantages, equally profitable both to the landlord and occupier.

The account of the orchards at Loose, near Maidstone, has this new passage in the Octavo: 'and there is a general neatness kept up here in the culture of them which is particularly noticed in the green clipped hedges round them, which gives the whole an appearance of a well kept cultivated garden ground'. Surely the freshness of this description can only mean that it is an eye-witness account of something recently seen.

When weighing the significance of these passages one must always bear in mind the facts that the original account would have been written anything up to twenty years before the new edition was prepared; that for at least six years Hasted had not been in a position to revisit any of the places; and that so far as concerns the villages in west Kent, of which specially lengthy new accounts appear in the Octavo, Hasted was unlikely to have seen them for a quarter of a century.

The village of East Farleigh gives rise to a type of purple patch appearing for the first time in the second edition: 'From the river the ground rises suddenly and steep southward, forming a beautiful combination of objects to the sight, having the village and church on the height, intersected with large spreading oaks and plantations of fruit, and the luxuriant hop, whilst the River Medway, gliding its silver stream below, reflects the varied landscape'.

In the same mood is the new description of East Barming. In his first edition Hasted refers to several small springs gushing from under the rock and running through the meadows into the Medway, but the more lyrical second edition has the stream running 'precipitously in trinkling rills', this after further references to spreading oaks and the Medway 'meandering its silver stream'. We read further that 'the fertility of soil, the healthiness of air, the rich variety of prospect, adorned by the continuous range of capital seats, with their parks and plantations, form altogether an assemblage of objects, in which nature and art appear to have lavished their choicest endeavour, and to form a scene teeming with whatever can make it desirable both for pleasure and profit. The church, standing by itself, among a grove of elms, the slight delicate white spire of which rising above the foliage of the grove affords a pleasing prospect to the neighbouring country'.

Coming to Aylesford we find that the new description in the second edition contains a typical piece of eye-witness observation: '. . . the hill on which the church stands rises so suddenly that the church . . . stands higher even than the tops of the chimneys of the houses below it'.

When we arrive at Mereworth, between Maidstone and Tonbridge, the Folio mentions 'a fine avenue of oaks planted on each side of the turnpike road' to which the writer of the second edition has added: 'with a low neatly cut quick hedge along the whole of it which leaves an uninterrupted view of the house, park and grounds of Lord le Despenser, the church with its fine built spire . . . and beyond it an extensive country along the valley to Tunbridge, making altogether a most beautiful and luxuriant prospect'. The remark about the hedge shows that the writer must have paid a recent visit. It is at Mereworth also that we hear about the martin cats: 'the same as those at Hudson's Bay'—not the kind of information, one would have thought, to be gathered in the courtyards of the King's Bench Prison.

The new account of Nettlestead Place on the Medway has a mass of circumstantial detail which could only have been obtained on the spot:

> The mansion appears to have been spacious and noble, equal to the respectable families who once resided in it, though now it is for the most part over-run with weeds and spontaneous shrubs, and bears with it every mark of that vicissitude and ruin which is the inevitable lot of the transitous labours of man, however his utmost endeavours may

have been exerted to prevent it. It is now made use of as an oast to dry hops, and for a labourer to dwell in, the occupier of the manor farm living in a modern house between it and the church . . . The groves of young oaks, elms, and other trees, planted along the borders of the River Medway, contribute greatly to the beauty of the scenery, which is considerably heightened by the rich gardens of hops, and the different dwellings and cottages intervening at frequent spaces between them.

In the parish of Hunton, also on the Medway, we read that 'in the drought of summer, from the heat arising from the soil, the reflection of the sun beams, and the quantity of large buzzing flies which continally assault you from their haunts among the oak branches, it is most disagreeable and unpleasant to the extreme, the only exception being when you are stationary under the thick shade of a spreading oak'. On the Isle of Sheppey we are told of pastures 'almost covered with large anthills which look very slovenly' and of the grotesque and unsightly appearance of the tubs placed to collect water from the church roof at Eastchurch.

Last, but by no means the least significant, of the additions made in the second edition which seem to be worth mentioning is this sentence about agricultural practices in the parish of Capel, near Dover: 'In this parish I first saw the shocks of wheat, whilst in the fields, all covered in bad weather with bass matting, to secure them from the wet; which I am informed, is a usual custom in this neighbourhood, though not much approved of by the most intelligent farmers in it'. This is indeed a strange piece of information for Hasted to have pulled out of memory's store for his second edition after so many years. And stranger still that he should refer to himself in the first person, quite against his usual practice!

The use of the slightly artificial expression about the River Darent 'meandering its silver stream' at Farningham becomes more significant when we find later on that it is used over and over again and applied in fact to every river in Kent—the Medway, the Stour and the Dour to name a few.

When we arrive at the description of Boxley, near Maidstone, there is an important milestone from the point of view of critical examination of the text. The newly written part states that to the eastward there is a 'wet *cludgy* earth'. This is apparently a rendering of the Kent dialect word 'cledgy', meaning stiff and sticky, and is never used in any passage which is demonstrably the work of Hasted himself, or to put it another way, it is never used in the first edition. In the second, however, it is used repeatedly, more even than the 'silver stream'.

At Teston, on the Medway not far from Boxley, we run into another favourite expression: Teston House 'being of white stucco' is described as being a 'conspicuous object'. This expression is so constantly used in the descriptions that it almost becomes a cliché. In the first edition Hasted used it once or twice but the new writer, if we adapt the words of Fowler's *Modern English Usage,* allows a form of speech that has now and again served him well to master him, and one finds that in parish after parish either the church or a gentleman's seat is so described, including some that do not seem to be conspicuous at all. Another expression, that we find again at Yalding, is 'spreading oaks'. Henceforth the new writer rarely refers to an oak without using this epithet. Not far from Yalding the villages of Brenchley, Horsmonden and Chart Sutton have these arboreal phenomena and this cliché is used profusely throughout the text. Another new expression which occurs frequently, though perhaps not so persistently as to amount to a mannerism, is the phrase 'clothed with trees'.

A modern writer has commented that 'one of the most interesting points to note in these [Hasted's] descriptions is the wildness and remoteness of so much of the county at this date'. This impression is due almost entirely to the work of the writer of the second edition who must have concluded that the wilder, more dreary and unpleasant the picture he painted the more interesting it would be to the reader.

Hasted occasionally describes a village's surrounding as being unpleasant. This adjective is used with monotonous frequency in the new edition, a typical example being the description of Halstow near the Thames estuary:

> This part of the parish lies on a level and open to the adjoining marshes which render it most unpleasant, and at the same time unhealthy to an extreme, the look of which the inhabitants carry in their countenances; indeed it seems so enveloped among creeks, marshes and salts the look over which extends as far as the eye can see that it seems a boundary, beyond which the traveller dreads to hazard his future safety. The whole of this parish excepting towards the marshes has a woody appearance, the shaves and hedge-rows being very broad round the fields.

At times it seems as if the new writer is arguing with Hasted, as at Staplehurst where in the first edition the village and its individual buildings are both described as 'pleasant'. The new writer seems to be saying: 'well if the village is the only pleasant part the rest must be unpleasant' and he therefore describes it as 'excepting the village of it, an unpleasant situation'. Likewise at Brabourne the new writer joins issue with Hasted: 'The village', says the first edition, 'is situated on the side of a wide and beautiful valley'. The second edition deletes the word 'beautiful' and says: 'it is an unfrequented place and from the soils of it not a pleasant one'. In describing Fairfield (on Romney Marsh) Hasted himself beats the ghost to the punch by describing it as a most unpleasant and dreary place. Not to be outdone, the ghost adds: 'and is seemingly the sink of the whole marsh'.

The new writer seems to have made a resolution to fill out the descriptions by stating in nearly every case whether the parish is healthy or unhealthy and the unhealthy ones seem to predominate in most areas of Kent. Other adjectives applied with great freedom are 'dreary', 'forlorn' and 'wild', often associated with 'unfrequented'. As the work on the *History* went on the editor of the second edition found that Hasted's descriptions in the Folio were becoming fuller as he proceeded so that there was little for the ghost writer to add except to pump in a stream of words like 'unpleasant', 'unfrequented', 'wild', etc., at the appropriate places in the narrative. Sometimes both views got mixed up together as at Stodmarsh, near Canterbury, described in the second edition as 'neither pleasant nor healthy; the village which is very neat and pretty stands on a kind of green'. Needless to say 'neither pleasant nor healthy' is the second edition contribution.

Nemesis of a sort did in fact overtake the new writer when he had the temerity to meddle with the description of Waldershare, near Dover. He would not know, of course, that this had been provided by William Boteler and to beef up the description he inserted the words 'a wild and mountainous aspect' which brought a complaint from Boteler to Hasted that in Boteler's opinion Waldershare was neither wild nor mountainous.

To sum up then, there are four main categories of difference which distinguish the writing of the additional passages of the second edition from that of the Folio. First and most obviously noticeable is the repeated employment of certain expressions, such as the dialect word 'cludgy' used to describe a certain type of soil. This word is never found in the first edition, and with Hasted's high and mighty ideas about his own social background it seems most unlikely that he would constantly use a word of such lowly origin in his dignified historical work. Only a little less significant is the repeated use of the literary mannerism about a river 'meandering its silver stream'. Secondly, there is the use of quite ordinary expressions such as 'spreading oaks', 'conspicuous objects', and 'execrable roads' which is made obvious by constant repetition amounting to a mannerism as defined by Fowler. Thirdly, there is the general attitude of pessimism and denigration; the use and over-use of the words 'unhealthy', 'unpleasant', 'wild', and 'dreary' amount almost to a mannerism and seem quite contrary to Hasted's general tenor of praise for the county of Kent. Fourthly and lastly there are the new purple patches such as are found in the descriptions of East Farleigh and East Barming which have a style quite foreign to Hasted's pedestrian and unimaginative descriptions.

We can distinguish two quite different types of new writing. In the earlier part of the new *History* it is stylish, impressionistic and cultured, at least to the degree of avoiding clichés and mannerisms, but little more than halfway through the first volume, at Farningham, the clichés begin with a description of the river Darent 'meandering its silver stream'. We are well into Volume II of the Folio before we come to the first use of the word 'cludgy' and from that point the mannerisms and clichés are piled on increasingly and persist until the *History* enters on the last part of Kent (other than Canterbury) to be described, the Isle of Thanet.

There seem therefore to be two writers, the earlier one generally speaking providing completely new descriptions and the later one amending and supplementing the originals. Where does the dividing line come between their territories? At first sight one is inclined to suppose that the first cliché indicates the arrival of the second of the two writers, but the 'meandering silver stream' at Farnborough is an isolated instance; the expression only becomes characteristic when it is constantly repeated. It may be that the first writer used it quite innocuously at Farnborough and the second man decided to imitate his colleague every time a river was mentioned, in which case the boundary line might be moved down to the account of Boxley, near Maidstone, where the first 'cludgy' occurs. Another possibility is that the more cultured man dealt with the first Folio volume and the cliché-monger with the remainder. So far these are few clues to the identity of these two writers. To avoid constant periphrasis in my own notes I have christened the second writer, from his repeated use of the word 'cludgy', 'Mr. Cludge' and I have found that the giving of a name helpful in envisaging him as an actual person. As the other of the two writers has failed to indulge in any comparable literary antics he has to remain anonymous.

There are two hints about Mr. Cludge's background: he evidently knew something about Canada since he mentions that the martin cats at Mereworth are similar to those at Hudson's Bay, and he is also familiar with Lincolnshire because he compares the bleak flat scenery at Iwade, near Sittingbourne, with that of the Fens; and there is no evidence that Hasted ever visited Lincolnshire.

If, as I am convinced to be the fact, the additional descriptions of the parishes, and the editing and supplementing of Hasted's original accounts where these are allowed to stand, are not the unaided work of Hasted, then this discovery is of some importance. Mr. Cludge in particular describes a different Kent from the Kent of Hasted, constantly emphasising its wildness, dreariness, unpleasantness and so forth, which has led some readers to visualise 18th-century rural Kent as being vastly different from the countryside of today. But even more important, these anonymous and unacknowledged additions to Hasted's work, if indeed, as seems conclusively established, they are those of other hands, create a wrong idea as to what kind of a writer Hasted was. From a dull and pedestrian collector and recorder of information he is turned into a writer coruscating with wit and descriptive power though at the same time disfiguring his narratives with monotonous repetition of cliché after cliché.

So much for the additions and alterations, but what is the relevance of the subtractions from the text of the Folio? It might well be argued that the action of abridging an account almost entirely by straightforward deletions is so impersonal that it would be impossible to build any credible theory to prove that anyone except Hasted made the excisions, at least from internal evidence. But this is not necessarily true, since even before any question had arisen about the authorship I had noticed the crisp and businesslike way in which the alterations had been made, and had commented that Hasted (whom I assumed to be responsible) would have made an excellent newspaper sub-editor. It is therefore possible to receive some impression of the characteristics of a reviser from the way in which he handles mere deletions. In the light of what was to emerge later about Hasted's characteristics as a writer, the clean and decisive sub-editing scarcely seems what one would expect from him; at least, if proved responsible for it he would rise in one's estimation. These reflections support the possibility that Mr. Cludge and his more cultured colleague may have had at least some hand in the trimming as well as in the embellishing of the former narrative.

In fine, the conclusions to be drawn purely on the *internal* evidence are that the second edition of the *History of Kent* is not the sole and unaided work of Hasted himself but is in part at least ghosted by two other writers one or other of whom:

> *possibly* collaborated with Hasted in reducing the historical matter of the Folio by about one-third
>
> *certainly* rewrote the descriptions of a large number of the parishes, and
>
> *almost* certainly revised and edited the descriptions of many of the remainder.

It remains only to consider whether this hypothesis is in any way strengthened or weakened by such *external* evidence as is available.

In his letter to Boteler of 9 August 1786 (*see* p. 35) Hasted describes the project of a second edition in words that are equally, if not more, appropriate to a text that was to be remodelled by other writers as to one to be revised by Hasted himself. He does not say 'I will abridge the text', 'I will rearrange the subjects', 'I will enlarge the accounts of the parishes', but 'It will be abridged . . . the subject will be new arranged . . .' and so forth. He also says that 'all tautologies and uninteresting matters will be removed'. It is surely unusual for an author to admit that a style and method of writing used in a work on which he is still engaged suffers from such blemishes. Significantly, all these expressions used by Hasted exactly follow the terms of the press advertisement of the forthcoming second edition, issued by Bristow, in which Hasted's name is never once mentioned. It sounds as if Hasted, when writing to Boteler, had Bristow's advertisement before him.[1] In another letter to Boteler (*see* p. 37) the historian refers to 'compressing it within the promised bounds, which I am happy to find *we* can do'. It was not his practice to use 'we' as meaning 'I'.

The first two pages of the preface to the Folio edition relate, in the first person, how Hasted came to undertake the writing of the *History* and similarly enumerate the collections of manuscripts and the public records that he consulted in compiling it. In the second edition these pages are entirely suppressed, as are a number of later paragraphs using the pronoun 'I'. Other passages are reworded to avoid this usage.

Taking the external evidence as a whole, the general effect seems to be an all permeating *evasiveness,* suggesting a determination by those concerned to avoid saying outright that Hasted will be personally responsible for the new edition. As a penniless debtor in prison he would be in a very weak bargaining position with the printer of the second edition, Bristow; he could scarcely assume the burden of paying for the printing, so Bristow must have taken the risk of recouping himself from the sales. 'I have made a most safe and beneficial bargain with him, of profit to myself on publication' wrote Hasted (*see* p. 35). Under the arrangements for the first edition which had proved so onerous and unprofitable to Hasted, he had made himself responsible for the cost of printing and had, correspondingly, complete control over the text. He arranged for a second edition even before he had published the fourth and final volume of the Folio, which later achievement must have been his main ambition and preoccupation. Compared with this, the second edition publication was a minor event, though providing much-needed financial relief for one for whom starvation was always round the corner. The new edition was a project taken on by the printer at his own risk. Bristow was paying the piper and Bristow was calling the tune, no doubt employing the ghosts to see that the book was shortened, modernised and made more popular. Hasted, who was already expressing weariness with the task of finishing the Folio, probably left the new version very largely in the hands of Bristow and his assistants. It is only when we come to Volume 7 of the new edition (corresponding to the beginning of Volume III of the Folio) that we have amongst Hasted's papers any letters providing material for up-dating the earlier edition. This may indicate that, after the first six volumes had appeared, Hasted began to feel that he ought to have more control over the product, but the emendations of Mr. Cludge were to continue almost to the end.

The second edition was, for Hasted, of greater importance to his finances than to his literary ambition and reputation. Undoubtedly more readable ('Mr. Cludge' and his colleagues knew what they were doing) it was both meretricious and mutilated. Because it has been reprinted, the second edition is the one with which the vast majority of Hasted's readers are familiar. But the Folio, and not the Octavo, is the true Hasted's *History of Kent.*

Chapter Ten

THE FIELD NOTEBOOKS

IT SEEMED THAT THE STUDY of the manuscripts in the British Library had exhausted all Hasted's known sources, and that the investigation was at an end. It was at this very juncture that a telephone call from a friendly genealogist, Duncan Harrington, informed me that on a visit to the Kent Archives Office he had been shown 18 notebooks in Hasted's writing which appeared to be the field notebooks of his perambulations of Kent, of which neither my friend, nor I, nor any person of our acquaintance including responsible members of the Archives Office staff, had any previous knowledge.

These tidings were both interesting and alarming. The interest is obvious, and the alarm was about the possible effects on the 'Cludge' theory. If Hasted had made and preserved, and taken into the prison, detailed notes about his visitations, then one of the assumptions underlying the 'Cludge' theory was removed, and if by chance the notes should turn out to be the source from which the additional descriptive matter of the second edition was obtained, then the theory would be blown sky-high. Hurrying to Maidstone I found that there were 17 notebooks with an additional index volume. All were in the hand of Hasted and were bound in limp calf and saddle-stitched in the manner of small booklets. The books were labelled alphabetically from A to R (omitting J). This is Hasted's description of the books, written on the title page of book A:

> *Itinerarium Parochiale Cantianum* being the *Parochial Itinerary of Edw. Hasted* made by him thro the several parishes of the County of Kent for the collecting of whatever was worth notice Local or Personal anyways relating to that County begun in the year 1764 and continued to the year 1788. With sketches, plans and other drawings of tombs, churches, coats of arms and many other matters observed in the course of his searching throughout the same in 16 books marked with the several letters from A to Q inclusive.

After a few visits to County Archives to make notes on the books, I decided that the only thing to do was to have the whole lot photocopied so that they could be studied at length and in detail at Canterbury. This took some time, but the dividends were immense; the copies have become a valuable stand-by for the Hasted researches in general. The books did not, however, entirely conform to the description set out above. The backbone of the collection was, indeed, an extensive series of uniform batches of information, parish by parish, comprising a concise account of the local charities and a brief description of the church—whether large and imposing or small and mean, the number of aisles and chancels, the type of steeple and the number of bells. This would be followed by an exhaustive list of the church's monuments and sepulchral inscriptions, and sometimes a few lines of description of the parish. But only a minority of the parishes were so covered; none of those included in F I, about 40 of those in F II, and none in F IV. Only in F III were virtually all the parishes thus dealt with. In short, Hasted had been progressively improving his methods, until first his accident (according to him) and then his enforced flight from the country completely disrupted them.

Fig. 10. Sketch by Hasted of a little shrine in Brabourne church (Notebook C, p. 62).

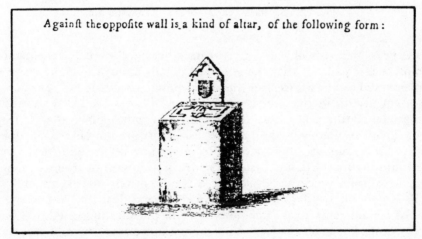

Fig. 11. The engraver faithfully reproduces Hasted's drawing (Folio Volume III, p. 302).

What use had the historian made of these voluminous details? Voluminous indeed, since an 18th-century church, from Hasted's notes, must have had its walls heavily encrusted and its floor almost entirely paved with tablets and inscribed stones. The answer is that he was not consistent about this; he started cautiously by mentioning only the charities and especially interesting monuments and inscriptions in his parochial descriptions; from this he graduated to a somewhat longer but still sum- marised account; finally (after he had progressed well into volume F III) he settled on the practice of setting out *in extenso* (in addition to the charities) a list of all the memorials in all the churches.

The next most noticeable feature of the notebooks are the long lists of 'Queries' under different parish headings. It seems that at the outset Hasted wished to be very methodical, and before visiting a parish to note the inscriptions and so forth, he put on his thinking cap and asked himself what were the outstanding uncertainties about ownerships of land, tithes, or any other matter needed to complete his account, so that he could ask about them while he was there. But so far as the record of the

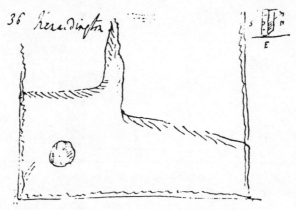

Fig. 12.   Sketch of earthworks at Kenardington
(Notebook B, p. 36).

notebooks goes, this system seems not to have been followed to its conclusion and it is in only a few parishes that the standard details about the church and charities are supplemented by the answers to the pre-formulated questions.

Almost equally distinctive are the many pages of notes headed 'Various Parishes'. These represented the use of the notebooks as commonplace books. Unlike the entries in the great albums in the Irby deposit, these are not entered in alphabetical order of parishes, nor are they derived from reading books and MSS.; they seem to record information obtained casually by word of mouth or from the newspapers. However, once again we notice that Hasted is not entirely consistent, and two brief entries in Notebook L relating to West Wickham and Seal (in West Kent) seem to be notes of amendments to the accounts of those parishes suggested by Lord Dacre. It may be recalled that letters from him suggesting various amendments to the text concerning Chevening were preserved by Hasted.[1] In other letters there were passing references to alterations to the history of West Wickham and Seal, with no details given. The hitherto missing information is now found, recorded for some unknown reason, in the field notebooks.

Typical events which attracted Hasted's attention were marriages and deaths in landowning families (here these notebooks seem to have been used in parallel with the great commonplace books in the Irby deposit), purchases of property and other recent dealings in land.

Notebooks M, N and Q are different from the others in that they contain material copied from books or documents and quite unrelated to any perambulation or visiting. Details of ecclesiastical leases are copied from a list compiled by Dr. Ducarel of the Lambeth library; abstracts of various legal documents in the possession of Bryan Faussett are included, and finally there are copious extracts from Holinshed's *Chronicles*.

To give some idea of the volume and variety of the contents, here is a complete list of the notebooks, giving the letter and the date (if any) inscribed on each, the number of pages and a brief indication of the contents. 'Standard information' means that mentioned above concerning the church and charities:

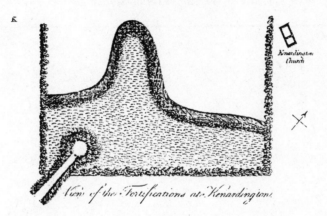

Fig. 13.   Engraving at p. 117 of Folio Volume III.

		Pages	Contents
A	1783	89	Queries. Standard information
B	1783	86	Standard information
C	1783	93	Queries. Standard information. Some shorter notes
D	1784	92	Standard information
E	1784	77	Standard information
F	1786	89	Standard information. Also additions to earlier descriptions
G	1787	64	Queries. Additions to earlier descriptions
H	1787	78	Standard information. Extracts from parish registers
I	1787	77	Standard information. Notes on 'Different Parishes'
K	1788	89	Standard information
L	1788	84	Standard information. Notes on 'Different Parishes'. Many entries probably made *c.* 1765
M	No date	41	Items from Lambeth and Augmentation Office records. Notes on 'Different Parishes'. Standard information
N	No date	42	Extracts from parish registers. Extracts from B. Faussett's papers. Extracts from churchwardens' accounts of one parish and miscellaneous notes
O	1766	82	Notes on 'Different Parishes'

Pages		Contents
P	1769 38	Notes on 'Different Parishes' and (with drawings) about Canterbury; glossary of Kentish Provincial words
Q	No date 36	(Final item dated 1800). Extracts from Holinshed's *Chronicles*. Miscellaneous notes
R	1788 71	Standard information. Extracts from parish registers. Notes about the Lade or Ladd family

Twice in the notebooks is found a list of 'General questions' which Hasted was reminding himself to ask, the two being almost identical:

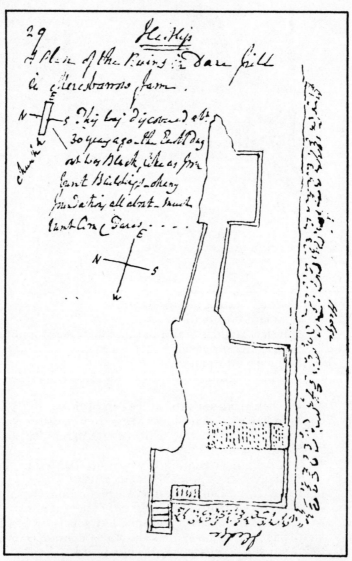

Fig. 14. Hasted's sketch of Roman remains at Meresborough,
near Rainham, from his field notebooks (I. 30).

Fig. 15.   The engraver's version of Hasted's sketch of Roman remains at Meresborough (Folio Volume II, p. 540).

What Manors or reputed so
What Courts held and rents
Gentlemen's houses
Hamlets, Boroughs and Constables
Separate jurisdictions
Shape, size and extent of Parish, if separated one part from the other
Antiquities as castles, ruins, barrows, coins, etc.
If any remarkable things
Natural history, plants, trees, shells, rivers, waters
Soil, situation and husbandry
Description of church and chapels if any
Glebe land and augmentation
Tithes due to parson and vicar
If any exemptions, or customs of paying tithes
Value of living; Patron and Impropriation
Charities, schools, almshouses, etc.
Register of Parish for families, memorandums and induction and decease
        of incumbents
Number of Houses and Inhabitants
Markets and Fairs
Trades, Mills and manufacturers

One plan of some fields and one drawing of an overgrown ruin are included although Hasted admits that it has 'slipt' his memory what they represent. Time and again entries relate to events occurring several years after the date shown at the front of the notebook.

No record made by Hasted would be complete without a sprinkling of practical hints, and these notebooks are no exceptions: on page 1 of notebook N there appear the following cryptic observations:

> Handmaid to the Arts
> Gum Arabic, sugar candy, equal quantities and Gumbouge—when dry breathe on it and then lay on it the leaf gold.

There is no explanation of the purpose of this no doubt valuable hint. On page 13 of the same book:

> (Deaths) July 31st (1778) Mrs. Balchen, wife of John Balchen, Esq., only daughter of George Templest of Angley in *Cranbrooke*.
> Sprits of hartshorn two or three times a day running wetted on a wart cures it.
> Frant House belongs to Mr. Fowle . . .

Unexpectedly, perhaps, one finds the death of the lady recorded (F III 47), the name being given as Balche*r*.

In notebook O, under the heading 'Different Parishes' (p. 19) there is the following strange account of a painful interlude in the relations between Archbishop Secker and the Dean and Chapter of Canterbury:

> Among the MSS. in the Library of the Dean and Chapter of Canterbury is a folio marked A 11 containing references to various records in different places. This book some years since was looked on as so valuable and to contain such particulars relating to their possessions that they refused Arbp. Secker the loan of it when he requested it, which he highly resented, in consequence of which they thought better of it and their Dean, Friend carried it up to London and went himself with it to Lambeth, but the Arbp. with much coldness refused to receive it on which Dean with many apologies requested only to leave it with His Grace, who remained silent upon which the Dean on taking his leave laid it down on a chair and departed.
>
> The Arbp. afterwards put it into the hands of Dr. Ducarel his Librarian, who being my very good friend brought it to me in Princes Court, Westminster, where I looked it over and made the following extracts. The above conduct of the Dean and Chapter shows not only their narrow jealousy but their ignorance, for there is not a single article in it that could anyways prejudice them or anyone else in the slightest degree whatsoever, or indeed be of any benefit or advantage to anyone.

Notebook P though dated 1769 refers to the purchase by William Deedes of Aldington Manor in 1799, clear proof that the notebooks must have been re-edited long after the date of their compilation. In the same notebook we have at the end a long list of Kentish provincial words, including this entry: 'Clutchy—Half-baked, doorwy'. However impatient we may be to be rid of the study of these notebooks, their strange contents continue to cry out for attention; for instance, on p. 31 of notebook Q there are some comments headed 'Philipott's *Villare*'. Now, in the cathedral library at Canterbury there are two copies of *Villare Cantianum* which have certain textual differences, though both purport to be the first edition (1659). Evidently Hasted had observed the same problem (he cannot have been using the Canterbury copies because *all* his remarks do not exactly fit them) and was noting the differences between two other examplars of Philipott's survey, and *some* of the variations he noted do in fact coincide with those between the two Canterbury books. This notebook ends with some Latin verses with a metrical translation by Hasted. They convey some fairly intimate advice about the habits necessary to preserve good health. And this effusion is dated 1800.

So where does all this leave the 'Cludge' theory? It strengthens it. None of the extra descriptive material added in the second edition originates from these notebooks. It is, therefore, even less likely than before that Hasted was responsible for obtaining such material.

Chapter Eleven

AN EIGHTEENTH-CENTURY MICROCOSM

SEVERAL OF THE CHARACTERS mentioned In Hasted's pages are found also in Boswell's *Johnson,* famous people like Gibbon and Wilkes, and local worthies such as John Cator of Beckenham and Mr. Longley of Rochester. John Nichols, Johnson's publisher, plays a part also in the Hasted story, as candid critic and as promulgator of Hasted's far-from-candid obituary, while Hasted's friend Astle lent books to the Lichfield sage, and had some trouble getting them back. Worth mentioning besides are the Austen family (relations of Jane), Warburton the herald, and Rowe Mores the antiquary.

Speaking of an industry which flourished in the Weald of Kent in the 16th and 17th centuries, Hasted remarks as follows:

> The occupation of clothier was of considerable consequence and esti-
> mation in those times, and was exercised by persons who possessed most
> of the landed property in the Weald, insomuch that almost all the ancient
> families of these parts, now of large estates and genteel rank in life, and
> some of them ennobled by titles, are sprung from, and owe their fortunes
> to ancestors who have used this great staple manufacture now almost
> unknown here.

Hasted then enumerates a string of family names, including the Gibbons and the Austens. How strange it is that these. Wealden families should have produced England's greatest historian and her most distinguished lady novelist. Edward Gibbon was a contemporary of Hasted, as indeed was Jane Austen, although her first book appeared only a year before Hasted's death. The only connection between Gibbon and Hasted's *History* is that Gibbon is mentioned in it as being descended from the Gibbons of West Cliffe (*see* page 132) rather than those of Rolvenden as supposed by Gibbon himself. Jane Austen is not mentioned, obviously, in the *History* but her brother Edward is, and three members of her family are among Hasted's correspondents. Her great-uncle, Francis Austen of Sevenoaks, had the honour of filling up one of Hasted's lengthy questionnaires about property descents since Philipott in various parishes in West Kent. Hasted tried unsuccessfully to get from Francis Austen (who was Clerk of the Peace of Kent) lists of deputy lieutenants and *custodes rotulorum.* Francis Austen did, however, manage to produce information about his own pedigree and about the Streatfeild family, Boxley Abbey, and Lady Falkland's estates. John Austen was of Horsmonden, the village from which the whole tribe originated, and was a cousin of Jane. He corrected errors and answered queries about the descents of his manors and the

Austen family. Another cousin, Thomas Knight, of Godmersham, supplied Hasted with a number of family pedigrees which are now with the historian's papers in the British Library. This Thomas Knight was of a family whose original name was Broadnax, established for many generations at Godmersham, but in 1727 the then Thomas Broadnax changed his name to May as a prerequisite to inheriting estates in Sussex. A bare eleven years later this gentleman again changed his name, this time to Knight to qualify for the inheritance of estates in Hampshire which included the advowson of the village of Steventon, to which living Thomas Knight presented his second cousin George as rector. The son of this Thomas Broadnax alias May alias Knight adopted Edward Austen, Jane's brother, and dying in 1792 left his estates to him. To complete the story Edward Austen in 1812, on the death of the benefactor's widow, took over the complete inheritance of the lands and changed his name also to Knight. The story is so complicated that one is chary of having blundered and made perhaps a false identification. It was therefore comforting to find amongst Hasted's papers a memorandum in his own writing, written in the 1790s, recording the death of Thomas Knight and his being succeeded by Edward Austen . . . 'the eldest son of George Austen, rector of Steventon in Hants'. It is no part of the Hasted story but perhaps worth mentioning that in after years Jane Austen often visited her brother at Godmersham and tradition has it that *Mansfield Park* was written at Edward's seat of Ford Park, Godmersham, which also provided the setting for the book.

'In the year 1768 . . . my mother . . . acquiesed in my persuasions for her to come and reside at Canterbury . . . Accordingly she entered into a treaty with Mr. Alderman Wilkes to assign over her lease of the house in Princes Court to him, and I finished it with him for her.' Thus Hasted, in his *Anecdotes* of the family. There is no doubt that John Wilkes, 'the friend to liberty', is referred to here. His biographer mentions that after a sojourn abroad, occasioned by his repeated clashes, with the courts of law, he returned to England, reaching London on 6 February 1768. He hired a house at the corner of Princes Court. In his correspondence with his daughter Mary ('Polly') Wilkes mentions, a little inaccurately we may suppose, that 'I cannot have my new house in Princes Court till midsummer for Mrs. Hasted's *brother* does not come to town till the 20th' (letter to Polly 5 June 1768). Although Wilkes did not become an alderman until 1769, Hasted's notes would be made long after Wilkes' election and the identification is quite clear.

Less clear are the events that occurred five years earlier, namely in 1763. In November of that year Wilkes fought a duel with Samuel Martin and suffered the wound which Thomas Astle refers to in his letter to Hasted of 19 November 1763. Although Wilkes was a very prominent man, the way Astle comes out with the news about him without any preamble makes it sound almost as if he was speaking of a mutual acquaintance. Then we have the unexplained reference to a Miss Wilkes who has entranced Sir Joseph Ayloffe, and in a second letter of Astle the sending of greetings to 'Miss W. if she is still with you'. I have quite failed to discover who this Miss Wilkes or Miss W. was. The 'friend of liberty' had a sister, but by 1763 she would probably be too old to fit the bill and in any case was probably married long before that year. Could the mysterious charmer then be 'Polly' Wilkes? Three facts make it virtually impossible for her to have been the lady; in 1763 she was only 13; she was lively and energetic but by no means pretty (*see* Zoffany's painting of Wilkes and her), and even more conclusive she was living in Paris at the time of the duel. As soon as he was well enough to travel Wilkes went to Paris to be with her and there is no hint in the correspondence between father and daughter that Polly came across the Channel at this time.

An associate of Wilkes was John Sawbridge, who succeeded him as Lord Mayor. Wilkes often visited Sawbridge at his seat in Kent, Olantigh, on the river Stour, nine miles above Canterbury. We recall John Thorpe's idea of touching 'the lord mayor' for a plate of Wye College (*see* page 58). The suggestion does not seem to have borne fruit since there is no such plate in the *History*.

Wilkes often came to Kent on tours of relaxation, and visited amongst other towns Canterbury where Hasted lived from about 1768. Having done business with Hasted and his mother over the Princes Court house did Wilkes, one wonders, renew the acquaintance when passing through Hasted's home city? The journeyings of the Wilkeses, John and Polly, to and from the Continent involved the Channel crossing via Dover. One of Hasted's familiar acquaintances was Peter Fector, 'a very considerable banker and merchant'. In a letter of 7 December 1764, dated from 'St John's Square', Polly Wilkes writes: 'We arrived after nine hours of sickness at Dover yesterday, where Mr. Factor was very polite and changed my louis for guineas'. This must surely be a reference to Fector.

The last Wilkes connection is that John owned and transferred to Polly the manor of Eythorne, just outside Dover. Hasted recalls the fact in his *History,* again without mentioning who the Wilkeses were. This treatment may be contrasted with that accorded to Sir Joseph Banks (*see* page 51) whose long letter describing his own exploits was transcribed in full into the *History*.

In the massive commonplace books that Hasted so laboriously compiled we find time and time again that the first entry regarding a manor (or other property) is a note of who owned it in 1725, according to 'Warb: MSS.'. Included in these books is a list of abbreviations, and one of the less attractive chores of the investigation was to convert this (or rather a copy of it) by use of scissors and paste into a rather more useful alphabetical version. This rearrangement showed up the fact that there were three different interpretations in the list of what was meant by 'Warb: MSS.', the first one being as follows: 'The MSS. papers of Mr. Warburton the Herald towards a *History of Kent* in the hands of Mr. Jacob of Feversham'. The name of Warburton crops up again in the manuscript Add. 5480 in the British Library (*see* page 133) in the sub-heading to many pages of sketches of Kent scenes 'taken by Mr. Warburton, the Herald, in his survey of the county in 1725'.

We can leave Warburton for the moment and give attention to Rowe Mores who first comes into the picture through John Thorpe's letters (*see* page 60). The same letter which introduces us to Mores also presents (and in no favourable light) John Nichols the printer. Nichols, it will be recalled, printed Mores' *History of Tunstall* and had taken the opportunity of contrasting it very favourably with Hasted's first folio volume. Then, in the British Library, we come across two manuscripts (Add. 5526 and Add. 5532) purchased by Hasted at Rowe Mores' sale.

These two documents had indeed a chequered history, having first been sold when Rowe Mores' intemperate habits threatened him with insolvency; they were purchased by Hasted and sold by him when his extravagances had resulted in his incarceration in the Kings Bench Debtors' Prison. When we read Warburton's biography we find there is an unexpected link; Warburton's son married the sister of Rowe Mores. In the light of Nichols' dashing attack on Hasted's first volume, it now seems surprising to recall Hasted's self-composed obituary and his request to his executor to use the kind offices of Nichols to obtain its publication in the *Gentleman's Magazine*. This quite complicated imbroglio might also be said to include the name of Thomas Astle since he engaged in correspondence with John Nichols in an attempt to prevail on him to take on the publication of Hasted's second edition.

Chapter Twelve

HASTED'S ANCESTRAL ESTATES

Rochester

ALTHOUGH IT PERTAINS only indirectly to his life's work as an historian, the story of Hasted's loss of his ancestral estates, and his eventual recovery of them, is one of the more dramatic ingredients of the legend that has grown up around his name.

Until 1972 there was some controversy as to whether his downfall was due to the expenses of the *History* or to his affair with Mary Jane Town, but in that year a new theory appeared in the Introduction to the reprint of the second edition where the loss of his lands is regarded as having been largely due to the activities of his solicitor, Thomas Williams. This gentleman is described as unscrupulous and unpleasant and compared unfavourably with Shylock. The 1789 crisis in Hasted's finances was 'just what Williams had been waiting for' and in the 'specious guise' of confidential adviser he succeeded in getting Hasted's estates into his own hands at an under-valuation. To obtain Hasted's reluctant assent to the transaction Williams offered to execute a bond undertaking to reconvey the estates if within a year the purchase price was repaid. This period the solicitor fraudulently reduced to six months 'knowing well that Hasted could not possibly find the money in this period'. The hapless Hasted was 'a child in the hands of the law' and was quite unable to meet the six months' deadline, so that Williams' nefarious plan seemed to have succeeded. But, years later, when Hasted was in the King's Bench prison, his son rediscovered the bond, and as a result Hasted was able, after proceedings in Chancery, triumphantly to obtain the Lord Chancellor's decree for the recovery of his estates, and also to secure his own release from prison.

That is the interpretation adopted in the Introduction of the events leading to the loss of the Hasted estates, but whatever the cause of their loss, no one questioned the fact of their ultimate recovery. After all, Hasted had affirmed it in his auto-obituary.

The theory that Thomas Williams was at the bottom of Hasted's ruin as a landowner is based on a statement in the latter's handwriting found in the Rochester Museum, formerly housed in Eastgate House but now in the old Guildhall. The Introduction had mentioned that in addition to this statement there was 'a mass of legal documents' which had never been properly examined. Even before my visit to the Rochester Museum to look at its Hastediana I had found these theories and assertions somewhat puzzling. This sale of the lands with an option to repurchase with six months, sounds to a lawyer very like a mortgage, because this was precisely the form of a legal mortgage up to 1926 when the conveyancing system was changed by Lord Birkenhead's legislation. The only difference was that the 'Proviso for Redemption' (which was, in effect an option to repurchase for the amount of the debt) was included in the mortgage deed itself, not in a separate bond, as had been done in Hasted's case. Another strange point was that Hasted said nothing about what was done to meet the huge debts that had necessitated the sale, nor did he explain why, if he had again become a well-to-do landowner, it was necessary for him to trespass on the charity of Lord Radnor to obtain a meagrely-remunerated and humble post in some almshouses in faraway Wiltshire.

The legal documents that Mr. Moad, the curator of the Guildhall Museum at Rochester, produced amounted to some twenty-five or so items which looked like an incomplete set of papers connected with some litigation. They included a certified copy of Thomas Williams' bond for the reconveyance of Hasted's estates, together with letters and valuations connected with the sale to Williams. There were two counsel's opinions, extracts from interrogatories, and comments on statements by opponents in the litigation and on answers to a Bill in Chancery.

Perhaps most important of all was the 'Statement of Mr. Hasted's Transactions with the late Mr. Thos. Williams concerning the Conveyance of his Estates to him and the Bond Mr. Williams gave him to reconvey the same'. In Hasted's hand, this contained, in addition to the special pleading that put all the blame for his misfortunes on Williams, the damaging revelation that before the sale to Williams and *without Williams' knowledge* Hasted had made second mortgages (then held by the representative executors of a Mr. Davies and a Mr. Rugg) of two of the estates transferred to Williams.

The counsel's opinions were supplied by J. S. Harvey, of the Middle Temple, an equity draughtsman and expert on property law who was later to become a Master of the Chancery. He it was who had written to William Boteler concerning his family coat-of-arms and whose letter had ended among Boteler's *Collections for Bewsborough, &c.*[1]

The first opinion, relying on Hasted's statement and the terms of the bond, was to the effect that there were strong circumstances why the conveyance to Williams should be considered in a court of equity as a mortgage only, and that, had Hasted applied within a reasonable time, though after the time specified in the bond, the court would have ordered the reconveyance of the estates to his trustees on payment of what was due to Williams. The long delay had weakened the case, but Harvey considered that success could be reasonably expected for such an application even at that late date. It was satisfactory to have this confirmation of the opinion that I had tentatively formed before visiting Rochester.

Harvey's second opinion, contained in a letter addressed to one Clarkson, a London attorney, refers to a proposed assignment by Hasted of his interests under the bond of Williams to Messrs. Simmons and Scudamore, attorneys representing the unsatisfied and indignant mortgagees, Davies and Rugg, on trust for their clients. Harvey advises that if the terms of the assignment were slightly amended and the document then executed by Hasted he would recommend the mortgagees to consent to Hasted's discharge from prison. The inference that Hasted won his freedom by passing away to the Davies and the Ruggs any vestige of interest that he might have held in his estates was indeed a new and surprising revelation.

I next studied the copy of Williams' bond. It is a most complex document, with long recitals (i.e., clauses beginning 'Whereas') having within them sub-recitals and sub-sub-recitals. It reveals that Hasted had transferred his estates to trustees so that the subsequent sale of the estates to Williams was, technically, made by these trustees, though Hasted joined in it. The purchase money—a mere £287 because of the many debts encumbering the estates—was paid to these trustees while the bulk of the sale-price was simply retained by Williams to meet the mortgage debts.

I had arrived at the museum at about 11.30 a.m. and after some three hours' work had examined, if only cursorily, and made notes on the papers that Mr. Moad had kindly produced. Bracing myself for what might be an unpleasant shock from the extent and difficulty of the task, I invited Mr. Moad to show me or give some idea of the nature of the remainder of the 'mass of legal documents' so dauntingly mentioned in the Introduction. 'But you have seen them all', replied Mr. Moad, 'there are no others'. Surprised but grateful, and having indented for photocopies of the more important documents, I went on my way, well pleased with the day's work.

Yet the mystery of Hasted's estates was by no means solved; in some ways it had actually deepened. What had happened as a result of Harvey's advice? Hasted had come out of prison, so it may be assumed that he signed the release of his rights, and from the tantalising references to Interrogatories and Bills in Chancery and Answers obviously some sort of litigation had ensued involving the Williams', but who else was concerned and what the result was could only be found out from the legal records themselves; and that meant going back to my old haunt, the Public Record Office, but this time on a more specific and definite inquiry.

Legal, not Literary

Having arrived at the Public Record Office I was informed that investigations of law-cases were conducted not in the Round Room but in the more humdrum surroundings of the Long Room. The familiar names of these rooms conceal their official titles, the *Literary* Search Room and the *Legal* Search Room respectively, to the latter of which I now repaired.

The first step was to decide what to look for, and where. In Hasted's day the organisation of the courts was much different from that of today. In addition to the tribunals administering the basic Common Law, like the King's Bench and the Exchequer, there were separate Chancery courts enforcing the rules of Equity, a code supposedly based on principles of justice as visualised by the Lord Chancellor and supplementing the common law. The mention of the Chancellor in Hasted's obituary showed that his suit must have been brought in the Chancery.

The Introduction had mentioned that before the discovery of Thomas Williams' now famous bond the attorney had died, and that his nephew John Williams was the heir to Hasted's former estates; accordingly, there should be in the Chancery records about 1802 or 1803 a case brought against John Williams ending with a decree ordering the reconveyance of part at least of the estates that had been sold to T. Williams.

A preliminary enquiry in the Long Room revealed that the pleadings in the case (the documents lodged by the parties setting out their contentions so that the court could understand what the dispute was all about) were filed quite separately from the decrees of the courts. The decrees are entered in a series of record books which are kept at Chancery Lane and are forthcoming after about three-quarters of an hour's notice; but the pleadings are stored elsewhere and it takes about a week or ten days to bring them to the Long Room. The registers, however, both of the decrees and of the pleadings are in the Long Room, but in neither group is a search as simple or as straightforward as might be imagined. For instance, to find the pleadings in a Chancery case one must search through each of six registers, one for each of the divisions of the court; and these registers are not alphabetical after the first letter—in other words all the H's, to take an example, are jumbled together haphazardly.

Despite the strong hint that Hasted might have assigned his rights under the bond, I first searched under his name in the registers for the years 1800–12 (the date of his death) but without result. The dates of the cases are those of 'sortation'—filing of the pleadings—and the staff of the Long Room advised that this might be a short time later than the date of the lodgement of the pleading. So without much hope I made a further search up to 1820. The additional labour was well rewarded, yielding no less than four entries under the name Hasted, viz., *Hasted v. Debary, Hasted v. Scudamore, Hasted v. Simmons* and *Hasted v. Rugg.* I requisitioned the pleadings filed under these references and returned on the appointed day to see what Dame Fortune had brought me. Each set of documents was, with a large number of others, wrapped in a canvas outer cover, and they together resembled a large roll of carpet which sprung open as soon as the cover was removed. Fortunately the scores of different pleadings were clearly numbered.

It was a great disappointment that the 'Hasted' to whom these pleadings referred was Edward Hasted, junior, the historian's son; but hope revived when a preliminary reading showed that the subject matter related to the father's affairs. One vital fact that transpired was that in 1803 J. P. Davies had instituted certain Chancery proceedings against John Williams *and against Hasted, senior.* No wonder I had had such difficulty in running the historian's case to earth; he was not the plaintiff, as he had implied, but a defendant.

Back, then, to the six-fold registers to look for *Davies v. Williams* and *Davies v. Hasted.* I found them both, dated 1803 and 1808 respectively. More waiting, and more carpet rolls to disentangle. *Davies v. Williams* was evidently the main case and *Davies v. Hasted* a subsidiary entry about the adding of more defendants to the main suit. The way ahead was now clear, a way that should lead to the heart of the mystery of Hasted's dealing with his estates.

The case of *Davies v. Williams* illustrates three important principles of equity which are still to be found in the text books—that a solicitor receiving benefits from a client who has no independent advice is guilty of 'constructive fraud'; that a conveyance of land with an option to repurchase may be considered to be a mortgage; but that 'delay defeats equity'.

The facts revealed, much abridged, are as follows. The executors of Joseph Davies and those of Robert Rugg (and their trustee-solicitors, John Simmons and William Scudamore) were suing John Williams and John Tasker (the executors of T. Williams), Sarah Williams, his sister-in-law, and a whole host of sisters, nieces and nephews who were beneficiaries under T. Williams' will, and lastly they were suing Hasted. The Plaintiffs were asking for the reconveyance of Hasted's former estates on payment of what (if anything) should be found due to T. Williams' estate, *to them,* Davies' and Rugg's executors. Their justification for this request took the form of a long and complex recital of the dealings with Hasted's former estates from 1784 to 1802. It seems that before his financial crisis in 1789 Hasted owned estates that were widely scattered in seven or eight country parishes around Rochester and Sittingbourne. The Plaintiffs represented Hasted's unpaid mortgagees who had lent him money on the security (as they thought) of certain of these lands in 1784 and 1786. Influenced no doubt by Hasted's version of the affair they laid the blame for their not being paid at the door of the wretched Thomas Williams rather than that of Hasted. The whole thing was a plot by Williams they alleged, to get hold of Hasted's estates at a knock-down price, and this was the way the wily attorney had set about putting it into effect; waiting until Hasted was so embarrassed financially as to be virtually clay in his hands, Williams persuaded him to transfer his estates to two trustees with instructions to sell them, pay off the debts from the proceeds, and hand the balance of the money to Hasted. Both the trustees were attorneys and, even more sinister, one of them was Williams' own nephew and partner, John Williams. Much of the money that Hasted owed was due (in mortgages) to clients of Williams, and the next step of the crafty solicitor was to pay these people off and thus get their mortgages into his own hands. Thomas Williams next (we are told) persuaded Hasted's mother to execute a document releasing Hasted's estates from the annuity which she had accepted in lieu of her claim as a widow or dower, i.e., a share in the rents of the estates. The way was then clear for Williams, taking advantage of Hasted's 'great distress', to buy his estates 'then worth £12,500 and upwards' for a miserable £8,685 plus £100. The bond for reconveyance within six months was then given. The holders of the 'secret' second mortgages, the Davies and the Ruggs, having no doubt heard that Hasted had sold out to Thomas Williams, applied to the new owner to pay the debts owing to them on the security of the lands transferred, but were checkmated by the cunning attorney who was able to plead that he had bought the estates in complete ignorance of the further mortgages, and as these were what are called 'equitable interests' he was not bound by them in any way.

Being ignorant of the fraudulent circumstances under which T. Williams had purchased Hasted's estates (went on the Plaintiffs' prayer) and also not knowing about the bond that Williams had given, Davies and Rugg were unable to enforce their claims, while Hasted in his distress mislaid the bond and considered it lost 'whereby he was less able to adopt proceedings to redeem the said premises'. But afterwards the Plaintiffs found out about the bond and they got Hasted's son to look for it. He discovered it at Hollingbourne amongst some old papers of his father and Hasted 'in order to enable the Plaintiffs to recover the amount of their demands, agreed to assign the benefit of the bond to J. Simmons and W. Scudamore' (the solicitors of the Ruggs and Davies). These two gentlemen were to endeavour to recover the estates and divide the residue between the two Plaintiff mortgagees. It will be noted that Hasted was to get nothing: the consideration for the transfer of the bond is apparent when we recall that after seven years in gaol he regained his liberty.

Reverting to the bill, the Plaintiffs asked that Hasted's transfer of the estates to T. Williams should be set aside, having been made for very inadequate consideration, by fraud, taking advantage of Hasted's distress and of his confidence in T. Williams as his legal adviser. Failing that, the Plaintiffs claimed that Hasted had least the right to get the lands back on paying what was owing to the Williams family, which right he had, of course, assigned to the Plaintiffs. The Williamses had been in possession of the estate for a dozen years and the bill went on to claim that they had already received enough money, from income and sales off, to discharge the mortgage debts owed to them. Finally, Hasted 'refuses to join your orators in this suit', and, since Chancery practice demanded that all interested parties must be brought in on one side or the other, he had to be made a defendant.

After this lengthy and complex bill in Chancery had been duly lodged and the creaking machinery had begun to take its course, the Plaintiffs made a discovery which must have shaken them considerably. In effect, they found that there were others with interests in Hasted's former estates besides themselves, Hasted, and the Williams family; these were the children of Hasted, who had claims under a family settlement made by the historian in 1789. We have already heard that Hasted had conveyed his estates to two trustees, giving them authority to sell them, pay off the mortgages, and hand any balance back to him. But this had been altered by the 1789 settlement and after providing for various life interests only one-third of the residue was to go to Hasted and the other two-thirds to his children, as he should decide. Hasted did not therefore have the undisputed right to make over the residuary interest to Simmons and Scudamore and, as the Plaintiffs put it, the children of Hasted 'pretended' that their title under the settlement was prior to any title the Plaintiffs could claim under the assignment.

To all this an answer was given in his pleadings by the Defendant John Williams which put the affairs in a somewhat different light. One of the Ruggs' strong points was they they actually had in their possession the lease granted to Hasted of Horsham Manor (one of the disputed properties). Williams retorted that Hasted had mortgaged the lease to one of T. Williams' clients to secure a loan, then pretended that he needed the document back in order to renew the lease from the landlords, and having got possession of it went off and raised another loan on it from the unsuspecting Rugg.

Set out in the schedule to Williams' pleading is a complete list of the freeholds and leaseholds which were in April 1790 conveyed to T. Williams 'with the situations, occupations, rents, or yearly value according to the rent book'. A photograph of this remarkable list (occupying most of two parchment skins) can now be seen in the Canterbury cathedral library.

Other points made by J. Williams were that in 1790 his uncle was no longer Hasted's attorney, having retired from the firm a few years before, and that his uncle paid off the clients' mortgages *after,* and not before he purchased Hasted's estates. John Williams' account of the circumstances in which Hasted executed the transfer of his estates has an air of candour and differs in many details from that given by Hasted. The overall impression is that the latter knew very well what he was doing, but was in difficulty because of his wish for secrecy. 'Hasted did not wish his desire to sell the estates to be known until he had left the country.'

In other words he did not wish to be around when the rival mortgagees discovered each other's existence. The purpose of the bond (according to J. Williams) was that it might be left in the hands of some friend or relation, in case someone could be found to pay more for the estates than T. Williams' price, so that the surplus could go to Hasted's family. In 1790 Rugg had brought an action against T. Williams claiming possession of Horsham Manor, but Williams satisfied Rugg's solicitor of his title and the action was dropped. Again, T. Williams had, in 1791, offered to transfer the estates to Hasted's mortgagees if they would pay Williams what was owed to him. This offer was not accepted but it seems to prove Williams' *bona fides.* As could be expected, J. Williams denied that the estates were worth £12,500, contending that they were only worth the figure his uncle gave for them.

In their answer, Hasted's children (Edward, junior, Charles, Ann, Catherine and John Septimus) said that they too desired the sale to T. Williams to be set aside, and claimed to have a better right to the estates than the Plaintiffs, mortgage or no mortgage, assignment or no assignment.

So much for the pleadings in the case of *Davies v. Williams*: now came the job of finding the court's decision. For this it was necessary to consult a different system of registers, not this time six-fold but (more trickily) involving reference to two successive registers to find any one reference. The whole process is even more complicated than it sounds; one recalls only that the second book has a turquoise cover and is difficult otherwise to identify, and that without the help of the staff on each occasion the searcher is liable to find, after an hour's wait, that he has indented for the wrong book. However, the decree was found eventually. It was made by the celebrated chancellor Lord Eldon and dated 24 May 1808. It is 20 folio pages in length. Before the actual decision there is a tedious recital of the various parties' pleadings, the mere gist of which has been stated above. We learn for the first time that Hasted had put in an answer, largely a repetition of his 'statement of his transaction with T. Williams' and therefore virtually evidence for the Plaintiffs by one who was supposedly a defendant. He too wished his conveyance to T. Williams to be set aside, but failing this the Ruggs and Davies' should be allowed to redeem the estates on paying the debt owed to Williams' estate. Hasted requested, as an alternative, that the estates should be sold to raise the money to pay the Ruggs and Davies' what was due to them. For himself, he had one modest plea: 'He hopes to be allowed his costs in this matter as he does not expect to derive any benefit for himself from this suit except the payment of the debts due to the executors of J. Davies and A. Rugg'.

Thus the preamble; Now for the decision: 'His Lordship doth declare', runs the decree, 'that the Conveyance to T. Williams ought only to stand as a security for what (if anything) shall be found due' on the taking of an account by a Master in Chancery, to John Williams 'for principle of the £8,685 mentioned in the Conveyance of the 7th April, 1790'. Other outgoings and all income received from the estates since 1790 were to be taken into account by the Master responsible, and John Williams was ordered to pay the entire taxed costs of the suits. Lord Eldon reserved all further consideration until the Master had reported.

To find out what happened next we have to go back to the case that we first discovered, *Hasted v. Debary*. The Plaintiffs were Hasted, junior, and his Chatham bankers, while the Defendants were various attorneys concerned in dealings with the former estates of Hasted, senior, his executor, Barlow, Harriet Taylor, the lady hitherto known to history as Harriet Brewster, Samuel Taylor, her husband, and sundry representatives of the deceased mortgagees of Hasted's estates. The gist of the case was that the Defendants, or some of them, were withholding monies due to the estate of Hasted, senior, to two-thirds of which the son claimed to be entitled. He had pledged his rights to the bankers to secure the £537 19s. 6d. he owed them and asked the Court to order payment after taking accounts and, if necessary, the appointment of a receiver.

In their pleadings the Plaintiffs repeat the whole sad story from 1789 to Lord Eldon's decree in 1808 (it was from this fortunate inclusion that it had been possible to trace the case of *Davies v. Williams*) and add that 'before any further proceedings were had in the said Causes' Hasted, senior, died. His will is mentioned as is the marriage of Harriet Brewster (his servant and residuary legatee) to Samuel Taylor. It is then revealed that after Hasted died in 1812 the principal parties to the litigation had entered into an agreement to settle their differences by a compromise. John Williams had computed that the balance due to the Williams' estate on account of Hasteds' debts was £13,931 11s. 0d. It was agreed that all the former properties of Hasted should be sold and the proceeds should be used first to meet Williams' claim, and secondly to pay off the Ruggs and Davies', the remainder going to Hasted's executor, Barlow, to apply as directed in Hasted's will. Two firms of London attorneys were retained to handle the disposals. 'Mr. Dawson, the auctioneer' conducted the sale of the larger part of the estates at the *Crown Inn,* Rochester, on 25 and 26 April 1812, and the attorneys disposed of the rest by private contract; the total realised was £22,816 5s. 1d.

Thus ran the Defendants' answer to the suit. They claimed that after paying off the mortgages they had 'only a small balance of £53 4s. 5d. A small number of sales had not been completed and were expected to yield another £3,000 or so. Hasted's executor had received only the bare costs of probate so that there was nothing at the moment to satisfy the claim of Hasted junior to two-thirds of the surplus, due to him in accordance with the family settlement and Hasted's will.

The final decree was not made until 1822, and it reads as follows:

Edwd. Hasted Clk & ors   Plts ⎫
Geo. Clarkson & ors   Defts ⎬ Tuesday, 19th Feby. 1822
                                          ⎭

Upon motion this day made unto this Ct by Mr. Beames of Cl for the plts. It was alled[c] that the plts having filed their Bill in this Court agst the Defts the mrs in diffce be[n] the part.[s] have been Accommodated. It was therefore prayed that the plts Bill may stand dismissed out of this Court wit[t] costs which is ord[d] accordingly Mr. Abercromby of Co[s] for the Defts consenting thereto.

J. C. (or I. C.)

The records of this litigation have obviously shaken the theory of Hasted's downfall being principally the fault of Thomas Williams. No doubt Williams was unwise to have any dealings with a former client without insisting on his being independently advised, but that seems to be the limit of his culpability. Hasted placed him in a fix by his insistence on an immediate solution of the problem of his debts before he fled the country while at the same time demanding complete secrecy.[2] Williams' valuation of the estate is on the file, based on the capital value of the rents receivable, and it is difficult to suggest what more he could have done to help his former client. Hasted, however, stands in a quite different light and must be held guilty of sharp practice (or worse) if only in his concealment of Ruggs' and Davies' mortgages from Williams. The attorney was thus deceived and he and his family became involved in unpleasant and costly litigation while the Ruggs and Davies' found that their debts were irrecoverable, until the ingenious Mr. Harvey came on the scene. Finally, Hasted bartered any interest he might have in his lands in return for the recovery of his freedom, yet did not forbear from claiming, quite untruthfully, that he had been defrauded of his estates but had later recovered them by the Chancellor's decree.

Chapter Thirteen

'FAMILIAR LETTERS'

THE SEARCH FOR THE TRUTH about Edward Hasted sometimes turns up facts that are unhelpful to his reputation. It is pleasant, therefore, to report the discovery of a circumstance highly creditable to him, namely that he is the author of a work, not unknown to writers of 17th-century biography, which has hitherto been credited to another writer, Thomas Astle. The latter undoubtedly assisted Hasted in the production of the book, but in a practical rather than a literary way, and Hasted modestly declined to have his own name on the title page.

The name of this book is usually rendered as *Familiar letters which passed between A. Hill and several eminent and ingenious persons of the last century*. Published in London in 1767, it is anonymous, but both the British Museum (now British Library) catalogue of printed books, and various articles in the *Dictionary of National Biography* (including that concerning Abraham Hill) name Thomas Astle as the author or editor.

The new discovery results from the observation of two facts, each quite neutral on its own, but very significant when considered in association. In Hasted's autograph list of his MSS. in the British Library there is an entry F. XIX 'Familiar letters to Abrham Hill Esqr. from various persons'. Hill was a learned and distinguished man, a charter member of the Royal Society, and on his retirement he settled at St John's, Sutton-at-Hone where, years later, Hasted lived for many years. The article on Hill in the *Dictionary of National Biography* asserts that a selection of his letters was edited by Thomas Astle 'from the manuscript in his possession' and published under the title mentioned above.

Hill's association with St John's, and Astle's use of the word 'familiar', echoing Hasted's title for his collection of Hill's letters, suggested an inquiry to ascertain whether the published letters came from Hasted's collection; in which case it might have been Hasted who had drawn Astle's attention to them.

The introduction to the book does not mention the source of the letters, merely stating that they had come into the writer's hands. Turning to Hasted's F. XIX (Add. 5488), it is noticeable that in spite of the title the MS. seems to contain relatively few letters addressed to A. Hill, and that such letters as there are can scarcely be described as 'familiar'; trade, money, legal matters, train oil and treacle are some of the topics. Item 56 is described in the MS. catalogue as a list of letters in the hand of Hasted. It is indeed in his hand, and consists of a single sheet of paper, folded so as to provide four pages; it lists 71 letters from 17 different writers, but includes none of those which remain in the MS. After particularising a large number of letters by giving the writer, date (sometimes only the year) and occasionally the place of origin, especially if abroad, Hasted proceeds to list the remainder of the letters in batches, giving only the name of the writer, but numbering them, e.g., 'Let. 17–21 inc. Walter Pope; Let. 22–28 Aglionby'. At the end of the list Hasted has written the name and address of a printer: Mr. Griffin, Catherine Street, Strand.

The implication is that Hasted withdrew the listed letters from the collection, and left a record of them in his MS. The obvious question is: 'Was there a connection between the letters on the list and the "Astle" book?' This was soon answered. In the Contents of the book each letter is itemised, and all 69 are easily identifiable in Hasted's list.[1] In some cases, the date, town of origin, and writer coincided; where Hasted mentions a batch of letters from one writer between certain dates, the dates and numbers of letters tally exactly, and moreover the sequence of the writers is often the same in list and book. Conversely, all but two of the letters appearing in Hasted's list are included in the Contents.

The number assigned to the letters are different in the list and the book; one reason for this is that certain letters about sea-fights with the Dutch, well down on Hasted's list, are given pride of place in the book, perhaps with an eye to customer appeal. The discrepancy at least shows that Hasted's list is not simply copied from the Contents.

Space does not permit an attempt to recount the subject matter of other letters; the writers, however, may be mentioned briefly. Two of them, Isaac Barrow, Anglican Divine and master of Trinity College, Cambridge, and Edmond Halley, the astronomer, were among the leading lights of the 17th century; of the remaining 15, seven, though less eminent that Barrow and Halley, have found their ways into the *Dictionary of National Biography*.

The text of the letters is preceded by a preface of 32 pages which is almost wholly devoted to a life of Abraham Hill. The writer (who significantly refers to himself as 'the editor' a practice familiar to anyone who has consulted Hasted's *History*) says that he obtained his information about Hill 'not only from his papers and correspondence, but from the mouth of one of Mr. Hill's friends, who died about three years since'. The friend is later identified as the Rev. Edmund Barrell, a prebendary of Rochester: '. . . the editor was particularly happy in the near neighbourhood and friendship of Mr. Barrell, from whom he received continual marks of kindness and regard . . .'. The preface contains a detailed and florid description of St John's, but makes no mention of Hasted's occupation and reconstruction of it. Hasted's list of his manuscripts includes a missing 'attempt towards a Life of Abraham Hill'.

The book does not mention that Mr. Barrell, in addition to his prebendal stall, occupied for some 59 years the living of Sutton-at-Hone. He died aged 89, and only such a long tenure of life and living could span the gap between the days of Hill (obt. 1721) and those when Astle and Hasted were flourishing.

The enquiries in the British Library showed, therefore, that it was virtually certain that the letters of A. Hill printed in the book came from Hasted's collection, and that it is highly probable that the historian was responsible for the preface. That does not leave much room for any contribution by Thomas Astle—advice in selecting the letters, perhaps, and general encouragement.

But this is not the sum of the evidence of Hasted's authorship. We may now turn to his letters to Astle already published in *Archaeologia Cantiana* XXVI (1905), p. 136, where there are references to some unknown publication in which both were concerned, of which the editor of the journal remarked 'We are unable to discover the nature of the publication to which Hasted refers'. Of this correspondence the items of interest are Nos. 10, 11 and 12. In September 1766 Hasted writes:

> I corrected the sheet you sent me and told the printer to send the others to me, but I have not heard from him since; by what you sent me I think there remains much of the letters unprinted. There is a paragraph in the first ten lines of the life, which I must alter before it is printed off, if I can do it in the proof sheet. You will be so kind to let me have it for that purpose, when read.

Most of the next letter, written in March 1767, is concerned with the publication. For convenience the passage is here set out again:

> I received the favor of yours on Sunday, with a very impertinent letter to you from Dodsley on the back of it. I have no great opinion of the merit of the letters myself, and yet I think I have seen more insignificant than these published, trifling as they are, he must be a most impudent puppy to offer to write such a one to you, a stranger to him. I am very sorry you have had so much trouble in managing of it, and did I not know your own worthy disposition and the pleasure you take in serving your friends, I should return you a sheet full of complaints for it, which I shall change into my sincere thanks to you, not only for this, but the many other acts of friendship I have so often received from you. The least trouble I think would be to let Griffin have it, clearing himself every expense, and if any profit should accrue from it, he should have the half of it; if he thinks that too much, then let him take the whole—in either case; that we should have 6 or 7 copies a piece half bound gratis—and that the title shall be approved by us before it is printed and neither of our names mentioned in or about it—as editors or otherwise—and if you will be so obliging to see this done, the sooner we get rid of it the better—for the time for the sale of such things wears off apace.

In a postscript Hasted adds: 'Whatever you agree with Griffin, make him sign his name to it'.

In the third letter, Hasted says that he is well pleased with 'your agreement about the letters', and continues: 'I hope by this time you have quite completed the whole of it: which I shall be glad to repay by any like good turn in my power'.

The dates in the correspondence fit perfectly with that of the publication of the book, and it will be observed that the printer Griffin, whose name is written at the end of Hasted's list, is referred to by name in letter 11. In the event, the book was printed by W. Johnston, but the change is not surprising in view of Hasted's hints of possible trouble with Griffin.

It is submitted that there can be no doubt that the 'publication' which the editor of *Archaeologia Cantiana* was unable to trace in 1905 was *Familiar letters addressed to Abraham Hill*. Hasted clearly thought that the undertaking was one in which Astle was helping him, Hasted, rather than the other way round, and the absence of the historian's name from the title page resulted from his own suggestion. There is no doubt that he was well entitled to have it there.

Chapter Fourteen

CONCLUSIONS

IN THE PREFACE to his first edition we may read in Hasted's own words of how he came to undertake the writing of a history of Kent. First, we hear, he collected materials 'without any further view, than that of affording me pleasure and employment, in my favourite search after a knowledge of former times'. He refers to the materials as 'my collection'. He would have allowed the use of them, he says, to anyone who had stepped forth to compile a history of the county. He refers to his 'literary pursuits', but without specifying them, and tells us that they brought him into contact with leading figures in the Society of Antiquaries, whose friendship and encouragement led him to consider 'carrying on the collections on a more extensive plan, and digesting them afterwards, with a view to publication'.

In 1757 Hasted went to live at St John's Jerusalem at Sutton-at-Hone, near Dartford, a historic seat which had come into the ownership of the Hill family, from whom Hasted rented it. The local vicar, Edmund Barrell, an aged man, had known the famous Abraham Hill when the latter lived at St John's many years before. We now know that Hasted came into possession of many of Abraham Hill's MSS. and much of his correspondence, some of which Hasted published in association with Thomas Astle. We have every reason to believe, moreover, that Hasted wrote a brief life of Abraham Hill, based on facts obtained from Barrell. It seems reasonable to suppose that Hasted's possession of Hill's papers was not unconnected with his friendship with Barrell, and that his preparations for publishing some of them and his composition of the short biography of Hill were some of the 'literary pursuits' which brought him into contact with Astle and others.

The wording of the Preface gives some hint of the methods he intended to pursue —more extensive collection, followed by digestion and publication—and we have many evidences in working papers and MSS. that 'collection' meant predominantly physical collection—the acquisition or copying of entire MSS. already existing.

We must never forget that the preparation of the *History* went on for a period of nearly forty years—from 1763 or earlier to 1799. The methods must surely have varied over the years, and the written evidence which shows in such great detail his means of gathering information for his last volume may not hold good for the earlier ones. Considering with this qualification the contents of the *History* and the evidence of the working papers we may now attempt to give some account of the processes by which the book was created.

The skeleton of it was provided by Thomas Philipott's *Villare Cantianum*. Here were listed the manors of Kent, with accounts of the descent of their ownerships down to the mid-17th century when the book was published. The manors Hasted chooses to describe are to a very large extent those mentioned by Philipott, whom Hasted cites as an authority hundreds of times in his book, and from whom he takes innumerable passages by verbatim copying. More flesh was put on the Philipott skeleton by taking matters from other printed books (especially those of Sir William Dugdale) and other sources, including pedigrees (collected like postage stamps or cigarette cards), and calendars and summaries made by earlier antiquaries.

Throughout the *History*, but more especially in the earlier volumes, there are numerous references to the 'Escheat Rolls', a phrase used by writers as a kind of shorthand expression for the records of the *Inquisitiones Post Mortem*. There was suspicion that Hasted had obtained his Escheat Roll references from secondary sources, and not from the original records (*see* p. 79). This was difficult to prove directly, and I had abandoned the attempt, when a hint that I came across in an old book encouraged me to try again. This time (*see* Appendix III) I was completely successful. The source of information represented by the Escheat Rolls had dried up in 1660, when the Court of Wards and feudal military tenures were swept away and to bring the story down to his own time Hasted was, therefore, thrown back on to his own resources. He used questionnaires (*see* page 48), systematic on-the-spot visiting and questioning, postal enquiries, and interviews, especially with family lawyers.

Philipott had made no attempt to give information about 'ecclesiastical jurisdiction' which figures so prominently in Hasted's *History,* but even without his help Hasted's task in this sphere would not be difficult; the established church was a continuing organisation, possessing full and detailed records, and he was encouraged and helped by one with an unrivalled knowledge of those authentic memorials, Dr. Ducarel, the librarian of Lambeth Palace.

When his narration approached his own time, Hasted was assured of help in overflowing volume by the human failing of vanity. The landowners and worthies of Kent, even such great men as Sir Joseph Banks and Lord Amhurst, inundated him with information about themselves and their families in order to immortalise themselves in his pages.

After work on the *History* had been in progress for at least seven years, a completely new element was injected into the work. Hasted moved to Canterbury and engaged himself in a vast course of new reading amongst the great historical works to be found in the cathedral library. His voluminous notes on these studies seem to have been used principally to add circumstantial decoration and footnotes to the main story.

After he had completed three volumes by these methods misfortune descended upon the historian and new expedients were required, as we have heard, to enable him to complete the final volume while living first in France and afterwards in the King's Bench prison. Fortunately William Boteler, William Boys and John Lyon were available to collect for Hasted the sort of information that he had hitherto himself sought out, and so the *History* was completed.

The most obvious faults in Hasted's work, narrowness of outlook and selectivity, stem from his methods. As 'Litterator' remarks in the *Gentleman's Magazine,* he

produced a history of Kent's squires rather than of Kent, and of squires as landowners rather than as men with activities in spheres other than the collection of
rents. Their achievements in art, science, literature, arms and administration are
hinted at very faintly.

Hasted made no attempt to link Kent history with national history. Exception-
ally, he made some references to the clothmaking industry in the Weald, but
generally speaking the great revolutions in social conditions and ways of life, the
improvements in methods of agriculture and in communications are mentioned
only casually, if at all. He was pre-eminently a copier and arranger of other writers'
works. He selected family seats and estates for attention in an arbitrary way.
Gentlemen's seats which had become farmhouses, such as Birchley in Biddenden,
simply disappeared from the record. Substantial properties and even whole hamlets
escaped any mention; the only test for inclusion was the existence of materials
about a given estate and if none happened to come Hasted's way the estate was
left in oblivion.

The book has, however, two great virtues. First, it embodies in some form or
another all the materials (including all the references in printed books) that Hasted
was able to discover in 40 long years of incredibly persistent searching and copying;
and secondly, it is extremely well indexed. It therefore gives a very detailed, if
one-sided, impression of the county of Kent and its historical records to its own
date, and provides excellent finger-posts for anyone approaching those records,
or any section of them, for the first time. So viewed, the question of its meticulous
accuracy, or otherwise, about which controversy has raged, is not of the first
importance.

When Hasted was living in the precincts of Canterbury cathedral in the early
1770s he probably did not know that some of his activities and foibles were being
recorded in a shorthand diary by an innocent-looking clergyman. The fact is that
between the years 1769 and 1773 the Rev. Joseph Price was keeping a secret
journal, the contents of which were decoded only a few years ago by a cypher
expert who identified the type of shorthand used by Price and managed to secure
an 18th-century primer of instructions in the system.[1] The excellent Mr. Price
made some notes about Hasted, who is referred to as 'a young antiquary'; this
at least would have pleased him, since he was nearly forty years of age. There are
many references in the diary to William Deedes, who is quoted as saying that
Hasted had found out about knight's service being exempt from gavelkind, and
called it in contempt 'Hasted's law'. Price observed that Hasted had 'as many
materials as would take up a long and studious life to arrange', and that the
historian was 'a most wrong-headed man'.

When it came to Mrs. Hasted (the wife, not the mother) the Rev. Mr. Price
resorted to certain cryptic outlines, the meaning of which remained hidden in
his breast and has never been successfully determined. Following the text-book
guidance, the nearest one can get is 'St. tches'. The entries describe Mrs. Hasted
as 'a miller's daughter who did not want to have him' and state, more obscurely,
that 'Beauvior [headmaster of the King's School] St. tches Mrs. Hasted'.

The reverend gentleman put his finger very accurately on the main sources of

Hasted's trouble, topics which are all too familiar to those who study his life-story: shortages of cash, which his marriage to the 'miller's daughter', or to use Hasted's own words 'a wife without fortune', completely failed to alleviate; defects of character which made him on the one hand quarrelsome and unpredictable and on the other, sly, deceitful and even fraudulent; and thirdly, lack of real aptitude for the task he had undertaken, so that he accumulated huge masses of information, a great deal of which was superfluous, and took an excessively long time and incurred crippling expenses in finishing the job. The result was that a project that a Dugdale or a Nichols could take in his stride became for Hasted an all-consuming lifetime obsession.

Financially and socially Hasted made a complete disaster of his life, but this was merely the price that he was willing to pay for attaining what he most desired, the title of 'The Historian of Kent'. The only people who had the right to complain of the justice of this exchange, his wife and family, are long dead, but the *History,* for all its faults, continues to be studied by generation after generation of the public.

Appendix I

THE MORE IMPORTANT OF HASTED'S MANUSCRIPTS IN THE BRITISH LIBRARY

(i) Heraldic Visitations

Add. *5507 (K. XLVI)*

Described by Hasted as 'A copie of the visitation Book of the County of Kent taken by John Philipott Rouge Dragon Annis 1690 etc. with the addition of sundry Pedigrees, Notes and Index'. We note that Hasted has carelessly put '1690' for '1619'. The entire document is over four hundred pages long, and on page 373 Hasted has the following note: 'I began copying this book Augt. 5th 1763 and I finished it September the 8th following'.

Add. *16.279*

This purports to be a copy of a visitation made in 1584, but Hasted has written on it a note to the following effect: 'N.B. Many of these pedigrees are continued down and I doubt whether the about [B.L. note 'above'] Date and Title is not put down in Error as it seems to me to be only a copy of the visitation of 1619'. The document is in Hasted's hand, but is not on his own list of his manuscripts.

Add. *5526 (Z. CXIII)*

Another copy of the Visitation of Kent by Philipott. Hasted purchased it at Rowe Mores' sale (1779). It is not therefore in his writing but in an old-fashioned hand, presumably that of Mores himself.

Add. *5532 (Z. CXII)*

A copy of the Visitation of Kent, 1574, purchased by Hasted at Rowe Mores' sale. The title (in Hasted's hand) states that it was 'Taken by Robert Cooke, Clarenceux King at Arms'.

(ii) Pedigrees

Add *5520 (X. CIII)*

This collection of 121 pedigrees, mostly in Hasted's hand, is no mere collector's piece, but a practical working document. In most cases the sources of the information is clearly stated, and the use of these pedigrees can be traced in all four of the 1st Folio Edition volumes.

To take a few typical specimens, No. 10 is described as 'Pedigree of Bathurst in all its branches approved by the late Earl of Bathurst for whose use it was drawn up by me E.H.'. It is a very elaborate document with drawings of coats of arms.

No. 16 is a pedigree of Smith or Smythe of Westenhanger and Bidborough 'Drawn up under the inspection and approbation of the late Chief Baron of the Exchequer and made from his papers and deeds, the heraldic visitations and other documents by me E.H.'. Someone has written in pencil: 'The part relating to the Lords Strangford is entirely wrong'.

No. 18 is 'A most curious and ample pedigree of Aucher copied by E.H. from one in the possession of S. Beckingham'.

No. 32 (Adye) is 'Sent by the Earl of Radnor' as are several others. A further number were supplied by Mr. Knight of Godmersham, who left his estates there to Jane Austen's brother.

No. 80 (Osborne) has a letter attached which is a reply to one which is in the Kent Archives Office (U 771 C 4).

No. 106 (Gibbon of West Cliffe) embodies the pedigree of the author of the *Decline and Fall,* communicated by Sir S. E. Brydges. According to this, the historian was descended from the younger branch of the Gibbons at West Cliffe, and not from the senior one at Hole in Rolvenden, as suggested by Gibbon himself in his autobiography.

Add. *5509 K. LVI)*

The pedigree of the noble family of Wotton, among which are interspersed those of other illustrious families.

Add. *5528*

Is a typical Hasted mystery. Although the title page refers to pedigrees of Kentish families 'collected by Edward Rowe Mores' and most of it is written in the old-fashioned hand which is presumably Mores', the document appears on Hasted's list as Z. CV. at the end and in slightly different writing thus appearing to be an addition after the writing of the main list.

Add. *5534 (Z. CIX)*

Pedigrees and arms of families in Kent down to 1781. Collected and copied by Hasted. They seem all to be of the more formal type with drawings of arms, etc.

(iii) **Exchequer, etc., Extracts**

Add. *5483 (E. X)*

'Transcript from the Escheat Rolls, Bundles of Reliefs, Aids, etc. down to the end of Queen Elizabeth's Reign.' This is a massive book of 404 pages in Hasted's hand. The entries start with a list of the knights' fees belonging to the honour of Clare, and include lists of tenants-in-chief and numerous extracts concerning fines. Trial samples show that some of the entries were used in the *History.*

(iv) **Miscellaneous**

Add. *5479 (D. IV)*

The first part is a copy of a document known as 'Church Notes taken in Kent', the work of the elder Philipott (*see Arch. Cant. lx* [1947], 50). The document from which this section was copied is now Egerton MS. 3310 in the British Library. The title of this section, written in Hasted's hand, is as follows: 'Notes taken of the armes, monuments, etc. in several churches in the County of Kent Begun to be taken in the year 1603 and to 1624. Communicated to me by Joseph Edmondson, Esq.'. The notes relate almost exclusively to coats of arms and monuments in a large number of churches in the county, including Canterbury Cathedral and its cloisters.

The heading for the second part of the manuscript is as follows: 'The following Notes, Coats of Arms, Drawings of Monuments and churches were copied by me from a curious MS. in the possession of John Thorp [*sic*] of Bexley, Esqr. in the year 1768'.

Lastly we have 'Some loose papers and memorandums all which I take to have been wrote by Peter Le Neve'.

Add. *5480 (D. V)*

Is thus described by Hasted: 'A Book Containing The Bearings or Coats of Arms of several of the Nobility and Gentry of Kent. Also Plans or Sketches of Tombs, Ruins, Churches, Houses, Monasteries, Harbours and various things of the same County and several Pedegrees [*sic*] and Descents of families belonging to it and other matters—Taken from the Several Printed Books of the best Authority or Curious Manuscripts Collected by E.H.'.

The document consists mainly of coats of arms of different families, many of them copied from what are described as Picard's MSS. An item of great interest is a long series of topographical sketches, including one of Deal Castle which is obviously the model for the engraving included in the *History*. Twenty-four pages of sketches with up to eight on a page are preceded by this sub-title: 'The following sketches of churches, seats, villages, etc. in Kent were taken by Mr. Warburton, the Herald, in his Survey of the County in 1725 and truly copied by me. E.H.'.

After this fascinating picture gallery the subject matter consists of pedigrees. Especially fine is the pedigree of Hulse, obviously a copy from some other document and described as having been 'collected out of the public records by John Taylor living at the *Lute* in Fleet Streete'. This is illustrated in full colour, including two pictures of knights bearing standards and shields. At the end of this pedigree Hasted has written: 'I begun copying this Pedigree of the Hulse's June the 20th, 1764 and finished it the 22nd instant following'. There are further sub-titles. One is: 'Lords, Knights and Gentlemen of Kent 1593. A Manuscript kindly communicated to me by Edw. Jacob Esq. of Feversham and Fellow of the Society of Antiquaries. Faithfully copied by me E.H.'. After a list of names there follow some hundreds of drawings of coats of arms, sometimes nine and sometimes 12 on a page.

Finally, writes Hasted: 'I began copying the MSS. about one at noon on the 30th June 1764 and finished it about the same time the next day'. One would have thought it was physically impossible for so many coats of arms to be copied out in 24 hours and we have evidence here of the incredible speed at which Hasted worked, which may account for his tendency towards inaccuracy. The final section of this MS. is headed: 'The several Coats of Arms in the Book of Picard the Herald Painter of Canterbury continued from p. 31' and terminates with: 'The End of the bearings taken from Picard's MSS. by me E.H.'.

Add. *5486 (F. XVI)*

A book containing sundry coats of arms, pedigrees, and monuments, observations on several churches, a chronological and heraldical diary and several views of houses and chapels. Coats of arms, pedigrees and descriptions of church monuments are promiscuously intermingled in this 47-page MS. in Hasted's hand. Some of the items that it contains are: 'The kindred and consanguinity of E.H. of Sutton in K. with Robt. Dingley Esq. of Lamienby in Bexley'; 'Observations in Sutton Ch. and church yard. Taken in Sept. 1764'; 'Heraldic miscellanies and other Events beginning May 2nd 1694 collected and carried on by Peter Le Neve Esq. Norroy King of Arms'; (1710) Account of the duel between Dering and Thornhill and trial of the latter for manslaughter, ending 'R. Neve 18th Jany. 1762'; 'This [MS.] was kindly lent to me by Mr. Edmondson of Warwick Street, Mowbray Herald Extraordinary 1764 and exactly copied by me, E.H.'. There are a number of pen drawings of buildings in the Darent area apparently made by Hasted himself and a like drawing of East Farleigh Bridge dated 1770.

SIXTEENTH- TO EIGHTEENTH-CENTURY ANTIQUARIES MENTIONED IN THIS BOOK

Agard, Arthur (1540–1615)

Exchequer official and antiquary. He spent much of his time making catalogues of the records of the Exchequer, and of state papers. Some of his work was printed by Sir Joseph Ayloffe, one of Hasted's associates. It is possible that some of Hasted's extracts from the Exchequer may have been copied from Agard's productions.

Anstis, John (1669–1744)

Garter King of Arms; published many learned works on such subjects as *The Honour of the Earl Marshall, The Register of the Order of the Garter* and *The Knighthood of the Bath.* MSS. of these and other works came into the hands of Thomas Astle in 1768, yet Hasted possessed many MSS. which had belonged to Anstis and are included in Add. 5485 (E.XV. on Hasted's own list).

Camden, William (1551–1623)

Antiquarian and historian. He published many learned historical and other works, and is of importance here as the author of *Britannia.* It was written in Latin and described as a topographical and antiquarian description of England, Scotland, Ireland, and adjacent islands. The first of its kind, the book became extremely popular, passing through several editions in Camden's lifetime. Hasted possessed a copy, but seems to have used more freely the *Magna Britannia* based on an English translation of Camden's book. Among other distinctions he held that of Clarenceux King of Arms. He was second master and later headmaster of Westminster School.

Chauncey, Sir Henry (1632–1719)

A lawyer and landowner in Hertfordshire who wrote a history of the county, published in 1700, the general form and arrangement of which Hasted tried to follow in his own *History of Kent.*

Cotton, Sir Robert Bruce, Bart. (1573–1631)

Antiquary; was primarily a collector of books, MSS. and coins. He helped Camden with the *Britannia.* He was proud of a supposed descent from Robert Bruce, and had the room at Fotheringay, where Mary, Queen of Scots, was executed, transferred to his family seat in Huntingdonshire. He was something of a politician and courtier. His library descended eventually to the fourth baronet, Sir John, who presented it to the nation. In 1753 it was transferred to the British Museum.

Dodsworth, Roger (1585-1654)

Collected materials for a *Monasticon* and a *Baronage*. These were used (with acknowledgements) by Dugdale for his works so entitled.

Dugdale, Sir William (1605-86)

Garter King of Arms. He composed a *History of Warwickshire,* a *Monasticon* (accounts of abbeys and their properties) and a *Baronage,* often building on foundations laid by the Yorkshire antiquarian Roger Dodsworth. The *History* is considered to be his masterpiece and is based on a plan copied by succeeding county historians, including Hasted. Other works included a history of St Paul's Cathedral and *History of Embanking and Draining.*

Edmondson, Joseph (d. 1768)

Coach painter, herald and genealogist. From painting coats of arms on gentlemen's carriages he acquired a knowledge of heraldry which he improved by study. He continued his lucrative trade after being created Mowbray Herald Extraordinary, while also receiving employment as an expert compiler of pedigrees. He wrote several massive books, including a *Baronage,* bringing an earlier work up-to-date, and a *Complete Body of Heraldry.* In composing these works he was helped by Hasted's friend Sir Joseph Ayloffe. Edmondson had another common interest with the historian in that the latter's fortune came originally from ornamental painting—of ships. Edmondson lent MSS. to Hasted to copy (*see* p. 134).

Glover, Robert (1544-88)

Somerset Herald; born at Ashford, Kent, the grandson of a baron of the Cinque Ports. He was only 27 when appointed Somerset Herald. A genius as a herald and genealogist, he was employed by other heralds to make visitations of the counties under their jurisdiction, including Durham, Cheshire and Yorkshire. He also attended missions to confer the Order of the Garter on foreign monarchs. He published nothing, but collected the information on which later writers made their reputations. Dugdale's *Baronage* was probably based on Glover's material, and he assisted Camden with his *Britannia.* Copies of many charters from Glover's collections were acquired by Hasted and one is included in ADD. 5485.

Leland, John (1506-52)

Antiquary. An accomplished scholar and royal favourite, he was appointed King's Antiquary—an office created for him alone. He spent some years making, on royal instructions, a survey of antiquities in the libraries of cathedrals, colleges, etc. He later became insane. The notes on his Itinerary were not published for more than a century and a half after his death. In the meantime, however, other antiquaries (including Dugdale and Camden) had used them in their own works. Hasted sometimes quotes Leland's descriptions.

Le Neve, Peter (1661-1729)

Norfolk antiquary, President of the Antiquarian Society and Norroy King of Arms. He made catalogues of the fines levied in Norfolk down to the reign of Henry VIII and helped Tanner with his *Monasticon* and other works. Hasted possessed some papers which he thought were written by Le Neve and copies of *Heraldic miscellania* collected by him.

Le Neve, Sir William (1600-61)

Clarenceux Herald. He was a trusted emissary of Charles I during the Civil War, but later went mad. Hasted possessed a MS. (now part of Add. 5485) from Le Neve's collections.

Nichols, John (1745-1826)

Printer, publisher and writer. He managed and wrote for the *Gentleman's Magazine* and published antiquarian and poetical collections, including *Bibliotheca Topographica Britannica*. An intimate friend of Dr. Johnson, he printed his *Lives of the English Poets*. Another friend was Edward Gibbon. Nichols specialised in publishing literary 'Anecdotes' (in the 18th century meaning of 'unpublished material'), and he was the 'Hasted' of Leicestershire.

St George, Sir Henry (1581-1644)

Garter King of Arms. There was a considerable tribe of St Georges who in the 17th century held high office in the College of Arms. One of Hasted's collections of MSS. Add. 5485 contained items from the collection of 'Sir H. St. George Clarenceux'. Sir Henry's father, Sir Richard, was Clarenceux, so that it is uncertain which of the two was referred to.

Warburton, John (1682-1759)

Hasted's 'Warburton the Herald'. A Lancastrian, he began his career as an exciseman, and was stationed (improbably one would think) at Bedale in Yorkshire. He was uneducated but very able as an antiquary, and in spite of his handicap became a member of the Royal Society and Society of Antiquaries, and also of the College of Arms (as Somerset Herald) where he quarrelled with the other members. He lost many valuable MSS. through his own carelessness and the ignorance of his servant who burnt them. He published archaeological works and maps of various counties in the north of England. His son married the sister of Rowe Mores, the antiquary.

Appendix III

HASTED'S USE OF THE PUBLIC RECORDS

THROUGHOUT the *History,* but more especially in the earlier volumes, there are numerous references to the 'Escheat Rolls'. This phrase was used by writers as a kind of shorthand expression for the records of the *Inquisitions Post Mortem,* which are thus described by Thomas Astle:

> These Records are preserved in Bundles, chronologically arranged; they are taken by virtue of Writs directed to the Escheators of each County or District, to summon a Jury on Oath, who were to enquire what lands any Person died seized of, and by what Rents or Services the same were held, and who was the next heir, and of what age the heir was, that the King might be informed of his Right of Escheat or Wardship: They also shew whether the Tenant was attainted of Treason, or was an Alien, in either of which cases they were seized into the King's hands; they likewise shew the Quantity, Quality, and Value of the lands of which each Tenant died seized &c. and they are the best Evidences of the Descents of Families and of Property.

On the face of it, if a writer offers as his authority (as Hasted frequently does) *Rot. Esch. ejus an.* ('The Escheat Roll of that year') one might think (there being no officially published copies of the rolls) that he had consulted the original roll or official calendar. In fact, many of Hasted's Escheat Roll references were obviously copied from the printed books he was using, especially Philipott's *Villare,* Tanner's *Monasticon,* and Dugdale's *Baronage.* There was a strong suspicion that most, or all, of the remainder were likewise obtained from secondary sources, in the shape of other persons' calendars (summaries) and extracts. This suspicion was prompted by four main considerations: first, that access to the public records at the time when he was writing was notoriously difficult and expensive; secondly, that the functionaries in charge of the records had for many years made a practice of composing calendars and making extracts for profit, and the results of their enterprise and labours were to be found in the possession of many antiquaries; thirdly, that Hasted's list of his manuscripts mentioned various documents that might well have come within that category; and fourthly, it was Hasted's normal practice to quote from secondary sources, as shown by his frequent references to the Harleian manuscripts as authority for facts which he most probably obtained from Wanley's catalogue.

The way to convert suspicion into certainty would have been to run to earth a manuscript containing calendars or extracts taken from the public records by a person other than Hasted, and to demonstrate that Hasted had access to such a document and had based his Escheat Roll references on it. This was a tall order, since all but one of Hasted's manuscripts which, from their descriptions, might have contained material extracted from the public records, are missing from his papers; they are some of the manuscripts which the trustees of the British Museum decided ('injudiciously') not to acquire at Hasted's sale.

There was, however, one exception—document number E. X on Hasted's list, which the trustees *did* acquire. It is now Additional Manuscript 5483 (*see* p. 132). It has over four hundred pages in Hasted's hand, nearly all devoted to extracts (written in Latin) from the public records from the time of Henry VIII to that of Elizabeth I. Convinced that the historian had not made these extracts himself, I obtained photocopies of the title page and a few other specimen pages. These I showed to the authorities of the Public Record Office and various academical persons in an endeavour to identify their secondary source. I was unsuccessful and was on the point of giving up the search when I came across the following remark of Henry Drake, the editor of a history of the Hundred of Blackheath, which purports to be a corrected, enlarged and continued version of the account in Hasted's *History*:

> Hasted has incorporated much of Philipott's *Villare Cantianum* verbatim. He borrowed extensively from Lambard, Kilburne and Harris, and noted every extract from the Lansdown MSS. indiscriminately under *Rot. Esch. ejus an.* As many of the entries noted could never have appeared on the Escheat Rolls, the practice caused some embarrassment before the source of his information was discovered.

It seemed that one had only to track down the 'Lansdown MSS.', and the secret of Hasted's Escheat Roll references would be revealed. Now, there are in the British Library two series of Lansdowne documents, the Manuscripts and the Charters. Are either of these the 'Lansdown MSS.' that Drake was referring to? There are two difficulties: these collections were acquired by the British Museum some years after Hasted was writing his *History,* and Drake had written of the 'Lansdown' MSS. (without an 'e'). Hopes rose when it was discovered that there was a substantial slab of Kentish material with the Lansdowne manuscripts, much of it collected by no less a figure than John Philipott, Somerset Herald. Yet the 'Lansdown' hunt proved to be otherwise unproductive—there seemed to be no obvious and direct connection between Philipott's compilations and Hasted's manuscripts or his *History.* This was discouraging, but the fact remained that, over a century ago, Henry Drake had concluded that Hasted's 'Escheat Rolls' references were not based on first-hand knowledge.

There was one resource remaining—to make a much more detailed study of Additional Manuscript 5483, the one Hasted document which remained of those based on the central records. To avoid incessant trips to the British Library, it was necessary to have the whole manuscript microfilmed and printed. The effort was indeed worthwhile, for the results showed that, so far from consulting the original Escheat Roll entries, Hasted did not even understand what the expression 'Escheat Rolls' meant! He used it to refer to items from the Patent Rolls and the Originalia, as well as from the Escheat Rolls themselves. In modern terms, he failed to distinguish between a report of a coroner's inquest and a record of a conveyance of land.

Perhaps an example can make clear what Hasted's practice was. On page 303 of Volume II of the Folio, we read that the manor of Yalding, having become forfeited to the Crown in the 13th year of King Henry VIII, on the execution of the Duke of Buckingham, the King granted it to the Earl of Worcester to hold to him and his heirs male *in capite* by Knight's service. The reference is *Rot. Esch. ejus an. pt. 3*. Add. 5483, p. 23a, has this entry (translated): 'The King has granted to the Earl of Worcester the manor of Yalding which was lately of Edward, Duke of Buckingham, to him and his heirs male to hold of the King in chief by military service'. (Reference 13 Henry VIII, pt. 3).

It seems quite certain that this is the source of Hasted's statement about the grant to the noble earl. Yet the item is actually taken from the Patent Rolls, the full reference being Patent Rolls, 13 Henry VIII, pt. 3, membrane 3. (*See Letters and Papers of Henry VIII,* Vol. 3, pt. 2, 2214-12.) It has nothing to do with the Escheat Rolls at all, and the reference (pt. 3) which Hasted copied makes nonsense when applied to those rolls. This example is only one of many; no wonder Henry Drake was embarrassed when he tried to trace the source of Hasted's Escheat Roll references.

But what does an occasional incorrect reference matter, it may be asked? We all make mistakes. But this one is particularly significant in its implications; it shows a surprising degree of ignorance on the part of Hasted about the nature of the different series of rolls, and even more importantly, it demonstrates very clearly that it was his practice to rely on calendars and transcripts rather than the original records. Had he gone to those records, he could not conceivably have perpetrated such a series of gaffes.

NOTES

Chapter One

1. The present tenants of St John's, the freehold of which belongs to the National Trust, have courteously demurred at the adjective 'injudicious', since they themselves have spent (with perhaps different aims) a great deal on improving the property!
2. 'From what hope have I sunk', a quotation from Terence. *See* more of these letters, p. 52.

Chapter Two

1. Some of Lyon's up-dating information was, I later found, also included in the Additions and Corrections to Volume IV of the first edition published in 1799.
2. *See* p. 39.
3. I was later to find that William Boteler's old home, Brook House, Eastry, had devolved eventually to a Mrs. Irby, whose maiden name was Boteler (information of the present owner, Mrs. W. E. Williamson). Presumably Dr. Boteler's papers passed in the same manner as the house.

Chapter Three

1. *See* p. 7.
2. The complete correspondence between Boteler and Hasted is the subject of the next chapter.

Chapter Four

1. A few earlier letters from Boteler, supplying information for FIII, have not been included.
2. Captain Harvey died of wounds received in the battle of the 'Glorious First of June', 1794.
3. He copied only one of Douglas's plates (*see* FIV, p. 246).
4. The maps are more fully dealt with later (p. 43).
5. *See* p. 4.
6. *See* p. 38.
7. *See* p. 57.
8. It actually predated the last volume of the Octavo edition by a few months.
9. *See* p. 37.

Chapter Five

1. Astle's calendars are in use in the Public Record Office to this day. Hasted certainly did 'take the benefit' of them, since they are the source-books for his Augmentation Office references.
2. John Sawbridge of Olantigh, Wye (*see* p. 112).
3. For 'Mr. Whitworth' *see* p. 75.

Chapter Six

1. In April 1768, writing to Mr. Woodgate, Hasted referred to 'a work I have employed myself in for some years, and have now nearly completed, which is an historical survey of this county of Kent'.

2. On the other hand, Dugdale's *Baronage,* one of the 'books which I have not', on which there are notes in the first commomplace book, is the source of a good deal of narrative here and there (e.g., the article on Tunbridge).

Chapter Seven

1. Also a typewritten copy of a letter written by an eccentric member of the Morrice family of Betteshanger (*see* p. 28).
2. *See* p. 51.

Chapter Eight

1. *See* Appendix II for biographical details.
2. They are briefly described in Appendix I.
3. This problem has already been noticed when considering Hasted's sources (*see* p. 79).

Chapter Nine

1. After these words had been written I obtained a copy of a letter (1 January 1796) addressed by Thomas Astle to John Nichols which referred to Hasted's proposed new Octavo edition. Astle asks whether Nichols would be interested in printing it. He mentions the intended abridgement of the work but says nothing of the rewriting of the description of the parishes.

Chapter Ten

1. *See* p. 63.

Chapter Twelve

1. *See* p. 19.
2. This precluded an offer of the estates to the public, which Williams advised.

Chapter Thirteen

1. The last letter is numbered LXX, but for some reason there is no LXIII.

Chapter Fourteen

1. The late Frank Higenbottam, sometime Canterbury city librarian.

INDEX